D0801621

Z

DATE DUE

TWAYNE'S WORLD AUTHORS SERIES
A Survey of the World's Literature

ITALY

Carlo Golino, University of Massachusetts

EDITOR

Giovanni Verga

TWAS 489

Giovanni Verga

GIOVANNI VERGA

By GIOVANNI CECCHETTI
University of California, Los Angeles

TWAYNE PUBLISHERS
A DIVISION OF G. K. HALL & CO., BOSTON

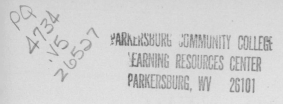
Library of Congress Cataloging in Publication Data

Cecchetti, Giovanni, 1922–
  Giovanni Verga.

  (Twayne's world author series ; TWAS 489 : Italy)
  Includes index.
  1. Verga, Giovanni, 1840–1922—Criticism and
interpretation.
PQ4734.V5Z6527   853′.8   77-19342
ISBN 0-8057-6330-9

MANUFACTURED IN THE UNITED STATES OF AMERICA

Contents

About the Author

Preface

Chronology

1. The Formative Years   11

2. Maturity: *Vita dei campi* and the New Style
   and Language   41

3. Maturity: *I Malavoglia*   68

4. A Drifting Interlude   98

5. *Mastro-don Gesualdo*   127

6. Twilight   141

Notes and References   155

Selected Bibliography   163

Index   167

About the Author

Giovanni Cecchetti is Professor of Italian at the University of California, Los Angeles, where from 1969 to 1977 he served as Chairman of the Department. He teaches courses on Dante and on Nineteenth and Twentieth century poetry and fiction. He holds a Doctor's Degree from the University of Florence, Italy. During the past thirty years he has been on the faculties of several American Universities, including the University of California (Berkeley), Tulane University (New Orleans), and Stanford University, and has lectured in most of the other major American and Canadian universities.

Mr. Cecchetti is the author of books on Giovanni Pascoli, Giacomo Leopardi, and Giovanni Verga, and has published studies on numerous Italian literary figures from Dante to 20th century writers, as well as on a number of modern English and American poets. He is a recognized authority on Verga, whose most representative short stories he has also translated under the title of *The She-Wolf and Other Stories* (University of California Press), and whose *Mastro-don Gesualdo* he is now translating. Finally, Mr. Cecchetti is known as a poet in his own right.

Preface

The works of Giovanni Verga's maturity constitute such an achievement as to place their author among the masters of modern European literature. Yet in the English-speaking world only a few people outside the small circle of specialists are aware of their existence.

In the 1880's, by putting himself—as he stated—"under the skin" of his characters, by "seeing with their eyes and speaking in their words," Verga devised a highly original narrative style and language. He omitted all purely descriptive passages as well as what could be suggested between the lines; and, most importantly, he told his stories in the very words of his characters—that is to say, he had his characters narrate themselves, without apparent intrusions on his part, thereby adopting in embryonic form a technique that years later would grow into the interior monologue. Through the resulting immediacy, directness, and powerful conciseness, his pages acquired an often purely lyrical quality. In the 1880's Verga was decidedly ahead of his time, but some decades later he came to be recognized as a precursor of modern fiction. His influence is discernible in young D'Annunzio, in De Roberto, and in nearly all twentieth-century Italian writers, from Svevo to Pavese to Pasolini. Even more significant is the fact that he gave artistic vitality to the theme (later to be newly and fully developed by Pirandello) of our living a ready-made role which is ultimately translated into our own identity.

The bibliography on Verga consists of nearly seven thousand items, yet no more than one, which is available exclusively in Italian, may be considered an extended monographic study: Luigi Russo's book (first published toward the end of 1919 and then reedited in the early 1930's). In English the only serious comprehensive essay remains Thomas G. Bergin's 1931 slim volume, which is a little too compact and is showing signs of age.

The purpose of the present book is to provide a more modern and more compendious discussion by offering a condensed analysis of all of Verga's works, while tracing the writer's development step by step: how he started writing, how he discovered his style, and how he could thoroughly grasp the plight of the poor and the down-trodden of his Sicily without being able to opt for, and to advocate, their social and economic progress. Thus the present book is intended as a critical guide to Verga's literary activity.

In order to give my discussion a solidly objective basis, I have made a constant effort never to lose sight of the works being analyzed. Hence the continual interweaving of plots and comments, with the result that the compressed summaries have become integral and inevitable components of the critical text. While I hope that this monograph will be understood and enjoyed even by those readers who have little knowledge of Verga, I would like it to be a point of departure for a better acquaintance not only with his works but with an entire area of European literature.

In the quotations from Verga's writings—offered in translation, as required by the series—I have attempted to preserve the crisp intensity of the original.

GIOVANNI CECCHETTI

Pacific Palisades, California

Chronology

1840   Giovanni Carmelo Verga, son of Giovanni Battista and Caterina Di Mauro, born in Catania, Sicily, on September 2.

1850   Attends the school of Antonino Abate, who encourages him
1858   to become a writer.

1857   Writes his first novel, *Amore e patria*.

1862   Publishes the novel *I carbonari della montagna*. His father dies.

1863   *Sulle lagune* appears in installments in the Florentine newspaper *La nuova Europa*.

1865   First of his extended visits to Florence.

1866   *Una peccatrice*.

1869   Moves to Florence, where he is befriended by many distinguished men of letters. His lifelong association with Luigi Capuana begins. Meets, and falls in love with, Giselda Fojanesi. Writes the play *Rose caduche*.

1871   *Storia di una capinera* is published.

1872   Moves to Milan, where he joins the group of local writers and artists. But from then on he visits Catania rather often. The same year Giselda Fojanesi marries Mario Rapisardi of Catania.

1873   *Eva*.

1874   "Nedda" and *Eros*. Writes *Tigre reale* (published in 1875).

1876   *Primavera ed altri racconti*.

1877   His sister Rosa dies.

1878   His mother dies.

1880   The great period of his masterpieces begins with the publication of *Vita dei campi*.

1881   *I Malavoglia* is published. He meets Countess Dina Castellazzi Di Sordevolo and falls in love with her.

1882   *Il marito di Elena*.

1883   *Novelle rusticane* and *Per le vie*. Rewrites the short story
1884   *Cavalleria rusticana* as a one-act tragedy, which is premiered in January 1884 in Turin. Meanwhile, Rapisardi discovers

that his wife is having an affair with Verga and forces her to leave Catania permanently. Publishes *Drammi intimi.*

1885   Writes the play *In portineria* by adapting the short story, "Il canarino del N. 15."

1887   *Vagabondaggio.*

1888   *Mastro-don Gesualdo* appears in installments in the *Nuova Antologia* (July–December).

1889   *Mastro-don Gesualdo* rewritten. The new version is published in book form by Treves at the end of the year.

1890   Pietro Mascagni's opera *Cavalleria rusticana,* based on a libretto derived from Verga's one-act tragedy, is premiered.

1891   *I ricordi del capitano D'Arce.*

1893   Following court litigation over the rights for Mascagni's *Cavalleria rusticana,* is awarded 143,000 lire (gold weight) as a one-time-only settlement. He accepts, but later alleges new claims, which are never considered valid by the courts. During the same year, after a period of indifference, his affair with Countess Dina Castellazzi Di Sordevolo flares up again. Now Dina is a widow—her husband having died in 1891. The affair will last for the rest of Verga's life.

1894   Resettles permanently in Catania.

1896   *Don Candeloro & C.*[i] and the two-act tragedy, *La lupa.*

1901   *La caccia al lupo* and *La caccia alla volpe.*

1903   His brother Pietro dies, of whose children he becomes the guardian.

1905   The short novel *Dal tuo al mio* is published. In 1903 it was performed in its original theatrical version, but had never been published as such.

1920   His eightieth birthday is officially celebrated, with Luigi Pirandello the speaker. Appointed Senator of the Kingdom of Italy.

1922   On January 24 is stricken with cerebral hemorrhage. Dies the morning of the twenty-seventh.

CHAPTER 1

The Formative Years

I From Catania to Florence

I N 1840, when Giovanni Verga was born, the city of Catania, Sicily, was a proud cultural center in the distant outskirts of Italian literary life. New trends and new books were examined and exalted, but they arrived late and could not escape being distorted by the provincial enthusiasm of the local would-be scholars. Catania boasted a university; but it might as well have been millions of miles away from the throbbing cities of Florence and Milan. Politically, it was part of the Kingdom of the Two Sicilies, under the Bourbons. Socially, it was a stronghold of agrarian bourgeoisie, still somewhat feudal and generally underdeveloped.

In Catania, Giovanni Verga, the son of a well-to-do landowner, was educated and spent the first twenty-five years of his life. There he saw the defeat of the Bourbons by Garibaldi and the annexation of the Kingdom of the Two Sicilies to the Kingdom of Italy. Without ever committing himself too deeply, he lived through the transitional period which was to be recreated a century later by Tomasi di Lampedusa in *Il gattopardo* (The Leopard).

In Catania, as well as on the rest of the island, schools were few and far between. Both the administrators and the teachers were priests. One of the exceptions, a lay man of letters, Antonino Abate, had founded a school of his own in order to support a large family. Soon he became the official teacher of the local young men who were preparing to enter the university. Around 1850 Giovanni Verga too enrolled in Antonino Abate's school. There he read Dante, Petrarch, Ariosto, Tasso, Monti, Foscolo, Manzoni, and the few other writers Abate considered essential to the mastery of the language. To the classics of Italian literature, Abate added the works of a local poet, Domenico Castorina, and some of his own writings.

11

Castorina's books, as well as Abate's, are bizarre in form and in content, overflowing with grammatical monstrosities and rhetorical emphasis, especially when dwelling on patriotic subjects, The latter were then not only fashionable, but mandatory.

The patriotism of the Risorgimento had come late to Sicily, as had the other manifestations of the Romantic era. Yet it produced a great amount of empty bombastic prose, which often consisted in repeating, imitating, and deforming the writers of the past. Antonino Abate and his school were particularly dedicated to such repetitions and deformations—if we are to accept the testimony of Federico De Roberto.[1] But in spite of the school he attended, it was during this period that Verga began to write, if only for the purpose of practicing what he had learned. At the age of fifteen he produced his first novel, *Amore e patria* (Love and Country), which Abate immediately praised to the sky. Verga happened to show the manuscript to his Latin teacher, the priest Mario Torrisi, who strongly advised him against publishing it. Thus the young man was spared the humiliation and the regrets he would have most certainly experienced later in life, had he followed Abate's advice.

Amore e patria tells a totally improbable story set against the backdrop of the American Revolution. Giulio Cattaneo defines it a collection of "senseless and frenetic events" and a "horrid melodramatic mess," written in an incredible style.[2] The general structure betrays the influence of Alexandre Dumas *père* (who was locally popular simply because he had visited Catania in 1835), and of Massimo D'Azeglio (a distinguished artist and statesman who had written some best-selling novels), as well as of Castorina and Abate.

In 1858 Verga completed his basic schooling and enrolled in the Faculty of Law at the University of Catania. But he did not like the subject, and soon began to write an historical novel, *I carbonari della montagna* (The Mountain Carbonari), which was published in 1860–61 in four small volumes. To defray the printing costs, Verga convinced his father to use the money destined for the last two years of his university education.

This time the action is set in Calabria during the reign of Joachim Murat, the king to whom Napoleon Bonaparte had given Southern Italy. The novel is not as "horrid" as *Amore e patria*, but the events are still improbable and the style no less turgid. Now, in addition to Dumas and D'Azeglio, Verga imitates also Francesco Domenico

Guerrazzi, who is famous to this day for his shallow sesquipedalian eloquence. An added source is Ugo Foscolo's *Ultime lettere di Jacopo Ortis* (Jacopo Ortis's Last Letters).

As an historical novel, *I carbonari della montagna* is not very historical. It is imbued with coarse and deforming patriotism. Murat, for instance, who had indeed been a very good king and had brought social and economic progress to lethargically undeveloped regions, is turned into a ruthless and bloody tyrant simply because he was a foreigner. In addition to being pseudohistorical, the work is also a pseudonovel. In it the author clumsily rehearses mostly themes he had found in his favorite readings and gives vent to some of his erotic fantasies.

I carbonari was never reprinted by the author, nor should it have been. In fact, Verga lived to regret having published it at all. Some scholars, such as Lina Perroni,[3] have scanned it to uncover and bring forth the portents of its author's future greatness. But their zeal has produced nothing convincing. Finally, and obviously for the same purpose, it was recently reprinted by Carlo Annoni, who has also provided a well-balanced introductory essay.[4] While this reprint may constitute a service to scholarship, it also represents a disservice to Verga.

In 1862, together with his friends Niccolò Niceforo and Antonino Abate, Verga founded a political weekly, *Roma degli italiani*. A few articles, including one by Verga himself, supporting universal military service for the Sicilians (who were still exempt), received the honor of being reproduced by some newspapers in continental Italy. But soon heavy disagreement engulfed the three founders, and within three months the weekly had to fold. Immediately, Verga and Niceforo founded *L'Italia contemporanea*. It lasted one issue. Then Verga, who never showed much inclination for the political arena, wrote another novel, *Sulle lagune* (On the Lagoon), which was published in 1863 in installments by *La nuova Europa*, a Florentine newspaper. The crossing of the Strait of Messina by having a book printed in what was then the cultural center of Italy must be viewed as a major event in the life of any Sicilian writer-aspirant. Also during that same period Verga lost his father, and from then on he remained deeply attached to his mother.

Sulle lagune is set in the Venice of 1861. The protagonist, a member of the Austrian garrison, falls in love with a Venetian girl

and goes through all kinds of difficulties because of her. The author
now uses a less implausible style. It is also significant that he substantially deemphasizes the patriotic themes, becomes interested in
contemporary life, and tries to portray the people he knows, with
their intimate desires and frustrations. Thus he begins to walk,
though still quite timidly, on the path of his novels of passion—
which, with all their grave shortcomings, must be viewed as a general preparation for his masterpieces.[5]

At this point Verga was growing restless. Since Catania and Sicily
had nothing more to offer, in 1865 he decided to visit Florence, then
the interim capital of the new Kingdom of Italy. There he was
dazzled not only by the brilliance of the Florentine society, but still
more by its cultural activities. His round trips between Sicily and
Florence became rather frequent until, in 1869, he took up permanent residence in the Tuscan city.

For young writers and ambitious men of letters from the outlying
provinces, it had been a long-standing custom to go to Tuscany, and
especially to Florence, for the purpose of cleansing one's own language and making it into a living, natural means of expression. In
the eighteenth century the great tragic poet Vittorio Alfieri had
moved to Florence in order to "de-Piedmontize" himself, as he
stated. Later Ugo Foscolo had followed in his footsteps, and so had
Alessandro Manzoni, who had gone there to revise the text of his
monumental novel, *I promessi sposi* (The Betrothed)—or, as he said
with a smile, to "rinse" his rags "in the Arno River." Manzoni, by
adopting almost the entire repertory of Tuscan expressions and
idioms, had been responsible more than anyone else for determining the language of modern Italian prose. Young Verga, in comparison to his predecessors, was a man of scant reading and of limited
culture. But he was full of enthusiasm and had a good ear. In Florence he met many important people and absorbed a fairly large
amount of the local language. The latter was to creep, however
sparsely, into all his books, even into the great works of his maturity. But it never completely replaced his expressive Sicilian background; as a matter of fact, precisely in the stories and novels set in
Sicily, together with some peculiarly Florentine expressions, many
words, inflections, and rhythms carry the flavor of the Sicilian
dialect. Thus we are inclined to conclude that Verga rediscovered
whatever was vital in the dialect through his contacts with the
Florentines.

II *Florence:* Una peccatrice

In Florence, where *Sulle lagune* had appeared, Verga did not arrive a total stranger. The city welcomed and encouraged him. Soon he completed his new novel, *Una peccatrice* (A Sinner), which was published in 1866 by Negro of Turin.

In this novel a passionate young Sicilian, Pietro Brusio, manages to conquer at once literary fame and the most beautiful woman. His love affair is frenetic and all-consuming. He enjoys his triumph, becomes deeply involved, gives and receives everything, until his passion slowly begins to fade. At the end of the novel, the "Sinner," Narcisa Valderi, realizing that he has tired of her, takes poison and dies on a sofa, after having made love with supreme abandon, and while Brusio plays on the piano the notes of a waltz evoking their sensual past. Brusio, broken in body and soul, withdraws to his small Sicilian town, to nurse his memories. In a sense, he too is dead.

The novel contains all the extreme ingredients of the late Romantic tales. It is repetitious and overextended, and it seems to have been written in a state of sexual delirium. "Voluptuous," "voluptuousness," "nevermore" are among the most commonly occurring words. In the introduction Verga declares that he has written of the omnipotence of love. In reality, he has put on paper his own most secret aspirations, has composed a piece of dream autobiography. Pietro Brusio, who achieves literary fame in a single stroke and conquers beautiful women to the point of seeing them die of love for him, is the projection and personification of what young Verga would have liked to be. In a letter to a friend, Pietro Brusio speaks of his life with Narcisa and says that he is "drunken with pleasure," totally immersed in a thrilling "feverish dream" (p. 80).[6] These last words ("feverish dream") may be taken as a definition of the novel.

Many years later, in 1892, *Una peccatrice* was disowned by its author, yet it has remained the point of departure in the history of the development of Verga's art. It is, in fact, the real beginning. Still, in the introduction Verga pretends to relate the circumstances that caused him to become acquainted with the substance of the novel. While riding in a coach, he was stopped by a funeral procession and was told that it was Narcisa Valderi's last journey. A young doctor, who had been acquainted with both Pietro and Narcisa, promises to send him all the documents—letters and even

photographs—connected with their story. At this point Verga tells
us that the novel is no more than the simple and faithful reconstruction of that story. Then he adds: "As far as I am concerned, I have
only coordinated the events and changed some names. . . . I have
only offered the naked narration and even reproduced some letters.
Of my own I have contributed nothing but the uniform color that
one may call the surface of the narration" (p. 12). Previous and
contemporary writers had often pretended to base their stories on
documents discovered by chance, or on eyewitness reports. Verga
himself will do so more than once. But it is interesting to note that
here, for the first time, he insists on conveying an impression of
authenticity, and goes beyond traditional expedients. He is still very
far, however, from the time when he will become convinced that
novels must be absolutely true to life, free of the inevitable deforming intrusions by the author.

For the purpose of discovering the signs of the future writer, all
the most serious critics have quoted from *Una peccatrice* in a variety
of ways. Luigi Russo, who authored the first significant monograph
on the Sicilian novelist, quotes the protagonist: "Fate! this is the
great word men cannot pronounce too often; yet I believe in it as
deeply as a Mohammedan" (p. 21); and comments: "It may be considered a conventional expression, but it will acquire profound re-
sonance and great implications for Nedda and 'Ntoni Malavoglia; the
tragic fatalism weighing so heavily on Verga's world was already
born."[7] Which is undoubtedly excessive. Additionally, the question
of Verga's fatalism calls for many reservations. In general terms,
fatalism may be uncovered in any work of art, for it lies at the very
core of events upon which man has no control, and which, almost
inevitably, determine the course of an individual's life. It is thus an
integral part of the human condition. But in *Una peccatrice* it hardly
exists—for there the mention of "Fate" represents something extremely frivolous and inconsequential, as is the case with so many
other words.

A more recent critic, Carmelo Musumarra, says that Pietro Brusio
is the first of Verga's "Doomed," and then he proceeds to show that
in the novel we can already sense the unadorned and essential
dialogue of the mature writer—once, of course, we purify the pages
from the empty and useless redundancies.[8] While the first of the
two statements may be acceptable, the second implies a totally
deceptive operation. In fact, if we rewrite even the most turgid and

bombastic piece of prose, we can reduce it to the essential, and then declare that it obviously contained the seeds of an extremely condensed style. The truth is that when Verga wrote this novel, he did not possess a clear idea of "Form"—or of expression—as one and the same thing with content. Gaetano Ragonese, on the other hand, finds the dramatic substance of the novel, as of all of Verga's first works, "in the clash between reality and dreams." Thus the male character is far more interesting than the female: he is vanquished by the very reality he tries to escape.[9]

In addition to the introduction, there is in the novel one theme that cannot be overlooked. Pietro Brusio undergoes sudden and incomprehensible changes of heart according to the changes in his financial condition. Thus, when his income vanishes, also his great passion cools off. He then says to Narcisa: "We cannot go on living as we have so far . . . without being rich" (p. 94). No matter how embryonically expressed, that is indeed a theme that will be taken up and developed again and again. Money has an extraordinary power in Verga's world. Human events, as well as human emotions, are governed by it as if by a ruthless god. The presence of this theme in *Una peccatrice* must be considered quite significant—much more so than Aurelio Navarria (the only Verga critic to remark on it) seems to think.[10]

III   Storia di una capinera

In 1869, when he took up permanent residence in Florence, Verga was thought to be a young man of great promise. This reputation made it easy for him to become acquainted with the best-known men of letters in the city. Francesco Dall'Ongaro, a highly regarded writer and critic, offered him all his help and encouragement. When Verga brought him a play he had written, Dall'Ongaro praised enthusiastically both its structure and the freshness of its dialogue, but could not manage to have it performed. Critics now believe that that play must be the posthumously printed *Rose caduche* (Fading Roses)—whose plot closely resembles the story of *Una peccatrice*.

Dall'Ongaro introduced the young Sicilian to all the writers who came to visit him: Aleardo Aleardi, Giovanni Prati, Andrea Maffei, Arnaldo Fusinato, the Russian revolutionist Bakunin, and a German Lady, Ludmilla Assing, who had written many books and was then contributing articles to a Viennese newspaper. In Florence there were also some of Verga's Sicilian friends: Luigi Capuana, a drama critic for *La Nazione*, and the bizarre poet Mario Rapisardi. In Dall'Ongaro's house Verga met Giselda Fojanesi, who was to become Rapisardi's wife and, briefly, his own mistress, and who was to bring him, forever cautious with women, the only stormy episode of his life. He also became friendly with the many artists gathered at the Caffè Michelangelo as well as with the singers and the actors who came to the city. During this period he vastly broadened his horizon and deprovincialized himself. He read many books and learned something about the theater and about music.

Since Dall'Ongaro had bestowed such high praises on his play, Verga thought of writing another; but first he decided to complete a new novel, *Storia di una capinera* (Story of a Blackcap), which was destined to be his only widely read novel. The fragile bird of the title refers to a girl confined to a cloister against her will.

The custom of forcing young girls to become nuns was some of the residue of feudalism, and was still very much alive in Verga's time—especially in Sicily. After Garibaldi and after the unification of Italy, the problem had turned into a burning social and political issue. In 1864 a book, *Misteri del chiostro napoletano* (Mysteries of Neapolitan Cloisters), by an ex-Benedictine nun, Enrichetta Caracciolo dei Principi di Fiorino, had aroused great indignation both in Italy and abroad. It was an age-old literary theme, to be found in many famous works of the past—such as *La Religieuse* of Diderot and the story of the nun of Monza in Manzoni's *Promessi sposi*—as well as in lesser but popular contemporary tales, like Tommaso Grossi's *Ildegonda* and Luigi Carrer's *La suora*. Even a relative of Dall'Ongaro's, Caterina Percoto, had written novels about frail young girls locked up in cloisters by selfish parents. But the main reason for the subject's striking a responsive chord in Verga is probably due to the fact that in his early years he had heard a great deal about cloistered women. Two of his aunts were nuns, and another aunt and his mother had been brought up in convents. The cloister of Santa Chiara in Catania was located almost directly across the street from his house. Federico De Roberto contends that *Storia di una capinera* was conceived one day when, during a lonely walk on the banks of the Arno River, Verga was besieged by the memories of his early years in Sicily.[11] But in reality, the novel is simply a tale of frustrated eroticism. Today we find it difficult to understand why it was widely read and heatedly discussed.

In the preface Verga tells us that he had observed a poor blackcap locked up in a cage and seen how sad she was when she watched the other birds fly about freely. She tried to accept her destiny, but could not swallow her food; finally she put her head under her wing and died. Verga continues by saying that when he heard the story of an unhappy girl imprisoned in a cloister, tortured by superstition and by unfulfilled love—"one of those stories that go unnoticed and yet are so common"—he thought of the innocent bird and wrote *Storia di una capinera*.

Due to a cholera epidemic, the protagonist, Maria, temporarily leaves her convent to join her family in the country. There she falls in love, but is forced to return to the convent as soon as the epidemic is over. Her young man marries her sister and, incredibly, the couple comes to live near the convent. Maria watches them embrace, her frustration forever deepening. Finally, she contracts tuberculosis, has hallucinations, is confined to a special cell, and there she dies. The novel allegedly consists of letters which Maria had written to a girl friend to relate to her daily feelings, and which had been delivered only after her death. This is more or less the same stratagem Verga adopted in *Una peccatrice* and is born of the same desire for authenticity. As Russo says, those letters are "turbulent, lachrimose, and gesticulative," and constitute "an unending and artistically aphonous soliloquy."[12] We may add that no rhetorical device can justify their style. And the characters never really come through: Maria is superficial and conventional, and the man with whom she is in love, Nino, remains little more than a name.

The difference between *Una peccatrice* and this novel is not great. In both cases the protagonists are women passionately in love, and in both cases they die when they realize, but cannot accept, having lost the men they love. In *Una peccatrice*, however, the male character is much more vigorous. The only progress we can detect in *Storia di una capinera* is a smoother and more polished language—certainly due to Verga's prolonged contacts with the Florentine environment.

Storia di una capinera was published in Milan in 1871, with an introduction by Caterina Percoto, who saw in it a work of social protest. Percoto's words, some phrases in Verga's own preface, and isolated expressions here and there must have convinced the readers that such was indeed the case. This may help to explain why it was widely read. Verga had written the novel in 1869, in one month. As soon as he had finished it, Dall'Ongaro promised to find a publisher. The young writer began to dream of how much he could write (at least one novel every three months) and of how much money he could thus make. Soon reality had to teach him that no one can write four novels a year, and that a good book requires a long period of incubation and years of hard work.

IV *Milan:* Eva

Toward the end of November 1872, Verga moved from Florence to Milan. He carried two letters of introduction: one by Luigi Capuana for Salvatore Farina, and the other by Francesco Dall'Ongaro for Tullo Massarani. Farina was then becoming a popular novelist, who wrote prolifically in defense of conventional bourgeois morality. Massarani was primarily a political man, well known and influential; but he was also a painter and a writer. Because of those two letters Verga felt immediately at home in Milan. Soon he met such writers as Arrigo Boito, Emilio Praga, Carlo Dossi, and many others. He became a regular in the celebrated salon of Countess Maffei—the gathering place for all the Milanese artistic world. He patronized the trattorias of the artists, especially Cova, where one day he met Emilio Treves, the man who was to be his publisher.

The Milanese were a lively group. They formed an artistic and literary school called *Scapigliatura* (literally, the School of the Disheveled, or of the Antiestablishmentarians), a sort of Bohème that tended on one side to recapture the themes and techniques of the early Romantics, and on the other to eliminate all "bourgeois" repressions, for the purpose of first living, and then presenting, reality as it is—even in its lowest and most squalid manifestations. Many of Verga's friends (but not Farina, a true "square" who preached dignity and integrity) belonged to the *Scapigliatura*. It is doubtful, however, that Verga ever considered himself a *scapigliato;* yet he profited much from his association with the group. He became better informed about the literary trends in foreign countries, was involved in numerous discussions on pivotal figures of his time, such as Baudelaire and Wagner, and learned that before producing a vital work one has to face, and solve, many problems.[13] Meanwhile, he kept applying the principles of his old formula, unaware that they were being imperceptibly changed by the unconscious insertion of new elements. In 1869, while still in Florence, he had begun *Eva*. He finished it in Milan on February 5, 1873, and managed to publish it toward the end of that same year.

Again the preface to the new novel insists on the veracity of the story, but now it limits itself to almost exclusively theoretical considerations. "Here is a narrative; it does not matter whether it is a story or a dream; what matters is that it is true, as it happened, or as it may have happened, without rhetoric and free of hypocrisy." Verga continues with a tirade against the insensitivity of the new affluent society and in defense of art—no longer the expression of civilization but simply a luxury. In those opening sentences many critics have read the beginning of a new Verga, of the writer who stands for realism and who is, therefore, well advanced on the road to his masterpieces. This is certainly an exaggeration, if not a total fallacy. What Verga states at the beginning of *Eva* may, in fact, appear to be little different from what he had declared in the preface to *Una peccatrice*—that he was simply relating the "naked facts" and actually reproducing documents. Should we, on the other hand, insist on discovering in young Verga a serious commitment to realism, to truth "without rhetoric and free of hypocrisy," we must then go so far as to acknowledge that such a commitment is also discernible in all his other early novels. This, of course, is possible—depending on what we mean by realism. Verga himself was convinced that he was analyzing and presenting "human passions" in their forceful reality. But, unfortunately, his pages remained shallow and stereotyped—far removed from the level he would later achieve. It cannot be denied, however, that *Eva* does represent some progress.

The story is supposedly told to the author during a ball by the male protagonist, Enrico Lanti. A young Sicilian artist, he falls madly in love with Eva, a ballerina who chooses him from a large number of suitors. When her profession keeps her on the road, Enrico becomes annoyed, and thus she renounces her career. She gives him all she can with the simplest and greatest devotion. But soon Enrico runs out of money, and the affair comes to an end. Subsequently, Eva becomes the mistress of a wealthy man whom Enrico challenges to a duel; his jealousy leads him to victory, but he is ill, and having lost all faith returns to his native village, where he soon dies of consumption.

Enrico Lanti is basically a very superficial character, almost a carbon copy of Pietro Brusio. But what makes the new novel entirely different from *Una peccatrice* is Eva. She is a simple girl with simple and uncomplicated aspirations. Her only dream is to love a man and to take care of him. Whenever she is present and whenever she speaks, Verga's style becomes sober and precise, almost essential. This is a direct reflection of her personality. Enrico Lanti, on the other hand, is always overemphatic and somewhat delirious. He intellectualizes everything. To him love is nothing but an uninterrupted series of frenetic embraces. Clinging to the provincial delusions of his Sicilian upbringing, he looks for triumphant successes and cannot accept everyday realities. As a result, he is defenseless and marches toward self-destruction, with self-pity his only company. The new and appealing character of Eva makes of Enrico Lanti a still greater artistic failure. Indeed, he may be viewed as the epitome of the rhetoric and hypocrisy Verga says he is rejecting. Only by creating Eva has Verga kept his word. Attilio Momigliano felt that Eva was Verga's first truly poetic creature.[14] This statement contains a great deal of truth—even though, in the general structure of the novel, Eva is stifled by all the surrounding conventional apparatus. Verga must have conceived Eva as a lower-level condensation of Ippolito Nievo's Pisana in the then celebrated *Confessioni di un Italiano* (The Castle of Fratta); but while Pisana's final degradation was her highest form of self-denial, Eva's decision to leave Enrico for a rich lover ("I have only my youth and must take advantage of it," p. 256), rests on the level of pure selfishness.

We cannot overlook some fertile themes in *Eva*, and first of all that love cannot survive the routine and the difficulties lovers must face when living together, without the constant nourishment of the obstacles created by distance and society. This was one of Verga's deep convictions—as we can learn from his letters and from his steadfast refusal to turn even his most mature love affair into a daily relationship.[15] As we shall see, there are times when he defends the union of married people, but not because of love (which is often nonexistent), but because it symbolizes the oneness of the family nucleus. Love itself is nothing but a short-lived luxury generated in the imagination and achievable through money.

After Eva has left him, Enrico Lanti reflects: "Love consists in a complex of circumstances. . . . I had loved her when my imagination and my heart could afford such a luxury." And he concludes: "Now I was hungry" (pp. 260–61). Thus the theme of the nondurability of love intermingles with the theme of poverty. A starving man does not have intense emotional needs. In the preface to *Eva* Verga takes issue with the affluent contemporary society for forgetting artistic creation and human emotions, but in the novel he goes on to prove the importance of money for both artistic creation and emotional expression. When Enrico Lanti falls into dire poverty, not only does he lose interest in Eva, but he quickly forgets all his artistic aspirations.

Also on another level Enrico Lanti makes some observations worth noting: "The contradiction existing in me between passion and feelings revealed itself in my works. I was false in art just as I was false in life" (p. 263). According to Giulio Marzot, with these words Verga was courageously declaring himself tired of the artificial world of his first novels and ready to tackle the human problems in a more profound and more genuine manner.[16] But it is difficult to agree with Marzot. When Verga put those words on Lanti's lips, he was not consciously announcing a program, nor was he rejecting the character he had created, as his following novels will demonstrate.

Eva was attacked as immoral by an anonymous reviewer in the *Nuova Antologia*,[17] and concurrently it was highly praised by one of the most authoritative critics of the time, Ferdinando Martini, who made some reservations on the "form," but for subject matter called it "one of the most beautiful novels among the many recently written."[18] Today, while acknowledging the freshness of the female protagonist, we cannot deny that the novel is turgid and full of easily datable commonplaces.

V Tigre reale *(Royal Tigress)*

This novel presents a Russian lady, Nata, who views love with the exclusiveness, the loftiness, and the subliminal selfishness of the mystics, as well as of the most conventional Romantic heroines. She is ill with consumption, but she wants to assure herself that after her death she will continue to live in someone's heart. While still in Russia, she had sacrificed everything for a man. But he had proved unworthy, and finally he had somehow redeemed himself by committing suicide. In Florence, where she lives mostly in seclusion, Nata meets, and falls in love with, a young Sicilian diplomat, Giorgio La Ferlita, but decides not to consummate the relationship for fear of losing him. Soon she leaves for Russia with the promise that she will return to die, "in silence" (p. 321), near him.

After her departure Giorgio marries a wealthy girl from his Sicilian hometown and, seemingly forgetting Nata, devotes himself to his wife, his children, and his vast landholdings. One day, he responds to a telegram from Nata and leaves home, where his son lies gravely ill. Nata forces him to spend a spectral, unreal night in her arms, and before dying makes him swear that she is the only one he ever loved. Upon his return home, Giorgio discovers that his son's life was miraculously saved by an emergency operation. Meanwhile, a cousin of his wife has just returned from the merchant marine and has rekindled old feelings of love in her. Giorgio, still totally obsessed with Nata, does not notice it. His wife becomes ill and, in the conviction that she is about to die, she confesses her emotional involvement to her husband. She recovers, and the two grow closer together. On the last page of the novel, while en route to his country estate, Giorgio is stopped by a funeral train, and when he reaches the estate itself, there is awaiting him a telegram with only one word: *Addio* (farewell).

Tigre reale is a strange and disjointed novel—certainly far worse than *Eva*. Nata is obviously intended to be a *femme fatale* for Giorgio, but the reader remains under the impression that she never has a real hold on him; for he appears almost incapable of complete involvement with anybody. Far less than in his previous works—where Verga had intended to make the male characters the protagonists, but in reality the women had become the truly determining forces from beginning to end—the female protagonist is the motor behind the action of the story.

Tigre reale has some other distinctive features. At the beginning of the second part, during the baptismal celebration of Giorgio's little boy, Verga puts all the men together in one room and lets them chat about women. What they say is not as relevant as Verga's technique, which represents a rudimentary attempt to delineate some of the people's personalities by means of their words. The results are still clumsy, but they may look like a distant anticipation of the mature chorality of *I Malavoglia* (The House by the Medlar Tree), where the characters narrate themselves directly, rather than through the words of the writer. Incidentally, the so-called minor characters in the novel may very well be the most successfully drawn: Giorgio's wife, her mother, and even Viscount Rancy. The latter, while advising Giorgio, throws in a bit of practical philosophy that could easily belong to Mastro-don Gesualdo: "We keep our heads on our shoulders, mind our own business, and look after our own interest" (p. 318).

The second part of *Tigre reale* grows from a moralistic assumption: once the family nucleus has been constituted, love passions must be quickly set to rest. If an old flame is by chance rekindled, it cannot be let burn. Both Giorgio and his wife personify this elemental social law; both have to shed tears of remorse as soon as they feel they have violated it. What they must care for is the child already with them, and the others who might come in the future. The little boy becomes very ill precisely when Giorgio is spending the night with Nata. Not only is this coincidence intended to make him obviously guilty, but it is designed to stress the principle that the family comes first and is, in fact, all-exclusive.

Although only in a few instances, the style of *Tigre reale* begins to be recognizable as Verga's. Here and there it is free of the characteristic turgidity of the previous novels. The following is a case in point. It is taken from the episode of the little boy's illness:

Signora Ruscaglia, who had learned much too late that her grandchild had taken a turn for the worse, finally arrived too, out of breath and all excited. . . . They were all crying as if little Giannino had already died. . . .

After the Doctor spoke there was a painful silence. Signora Ruscaglia was crying all by herself on the couch; the Doctor walked slowly up and down the room; Erminia, seated at the foot of the bed, her eyes fixed on her child, did not move; Carlo was standing next to her, leaning against the column of the bed, without breathing a word either (p. 347).

Rarely could young Verga present so large a group in so few words and with such subdued colors. We still read *Tigre reale* both because of such passages and because in it Verga tries to save the genuine and lasting social values at the expense of the sterile egotism which is destined to disappear without a trace—and which is incarnated in Nata, who, like all aristocrats, can only consume without giving, and therefore must die alone, at once ignorant of life and rejected by it.

VI Eros

Under this heading we might be tempted to group all of Verga's early works. Yet, in spite of the title, the concluding novel of the series is relatively free of the frenetic and delirious eroticism so prevalent in the others. This does not imply that passion remains absent, but the author seems to concentrate on the search for real and mature love, and on the resulting near impossibility of finding it, rather than on sensual frenzy.

No one knows exactly when *Eros* was written. All we know is that

it was printed in 1874, before *Tigre reale* and after "Nedda." Its style
and complexity, as well as its unusually large number of characters,
reveal a more experienced writer than the author of *Tigre reale*, but
the subject matter does not appear as consonant with Verga's personal inclinations as that of "Nedda." It stands out as the best of
Verga's Florentine novels—so called not necessarily because written in Florence, but because the action is mainly set in that city, or
in its surrounding area.

In *Eros* the novelist commits himself to exploring a certain type of
psychology. As is clear from the first chapter—a brief and incisive
presentation of the background of the story—he follows the then
fashionable positivistic and deterministic principles of cause and
effect. There the old Marquis Alberti is taking permanent leave of
his wife on the grounds that she has had an affair with Count Orlandi, and stipulates that she will care for their son's upbringing at
least until he is seven. The dialogue is reticent and overflowing with
the hypocrisy that is typical of Verga's aristocrats when they have
something very difficult and thorny to say to each other—a hypocrisy normally hidden behind such high-sounding words as dignity
and self respect. The child, Alberto Alberti, is entrusted to the
Collegio Cicognini, an exclusive boarding school in Prato. Soon both
his father and mother are dead and the young marquis grows up
alone, in an impersonal environment, withdrawn into a world of
fantasies.

This premise is obviously extremely important to the development of the story. It makes it possible for us to suspect that Alberto
will have difficulty accepting the realities of life and love. Being the
product of a destroyed family, he will have to march toward his own
destruction. He will be self-centered, egotistical, and will cause
untold misery to the woman eventually sharing his days and his
nights. And when he finally realizes that true love may indeed exist,
that his entire life has been a series of errors, this very realization
will crush him and bring him to suicide. With this novel Verga
accepted a great challenge: to call upon all the experience he had
accumulated and at the same time to explore a world crowded with
people he did not find congenial.

At the age of twenty Alberto leaves the boarding school to move
to a villa near Pistoia with his uncle, Bartolomeo Forlani, who is
administering his estates. There Alberto meets his cousin Adele, an

unselfish young woman capable of deep feelings, and her girl friend, Velleda Manfredini, a proud and egocentric person. He thinks he falls in love with Adele and becomes engaged to her. As a result, Velleda decides to leave the villa, but on her last night Alberto declares his love for her. Adele overhears the conversation and frees Alberto so that he can marry Velleda.

The scene shifts to Florence where both Alberto and Velleda have now moved. There Alberto is attracted to Countess Orlandi, the wife of Alberto's mother's ex-lover, and Velleda accepts the courtship of Prince Ferdinando Metelliani, whom she eventually marries, while Alberto follows the Countess to Lake Como. One night Alberto is surprised at the villa by Count Orlandi, who refuses to shoot him, for in the affair he sees some sort of poetic justice. He says: "Marquis Alberti, tonight I could shoot you like a thief. . . . But I do not feel I really can. Perhaps someday you'll find out why . . . you'll also find out that we are even" (p. 146).[19]

Here ends the first part, a complete and rather good novelette in its own right. Although the framework is somewhat artificial (the two Orlandi-Alberti love affairs), it has some superb pages. Whenever he writes about Adele and Uncle Bartolomeo, Verga shows a particularly happy hand. The character of Alberto, on the other hand, may leave us dissatisfied; it gives the impression of remaining almost undeveloped, as if Verga himself had not perceived all its potentialities.

From now on the novel proceeds almost by force of gravity. Following the Orlandi incident, Alberto travels alone to many parts of the world and supposedly becomes more and more cynical and corrupt. Twenty years later he happens to meet Adele in Florence, still unmarried and still faithful to her first love. The two have a long talk, in a dialogue which Verga must have considered of fundamental importance. In it, in fact, he tries to strike a balance between the cynical and the profoundly, if reticently, passionate. But he fails: in a Herculean effort to bridge a very long span of time for the purpose of bringing to the same level of communication two people who have travelled widely divergent roads, he ends up by composing a hurried, synoptic piece. On the surface he appears to be creating a psychologically plausible link between past and present, yet we cannot escape the belief that he has engineered all that dialogue merely for the purpose of having Alberto declare his philosophy:

I have seen through human nature as clearly as through a glass: we manufac-
ture most of our suffering by ourselves. We poison the feast of our youth by
exaggerating and complicating the pleasures of love to the point of turning
them into tortures, and we soil the serenity of our old age with the ghosts of
another life no one knows. *This* is the result of our civilization. . . . The
whole science of life consists in simplifying human passions, and in reducing
them to their natural proportions" (pp. 164–65).

Frankly we do not know whether these are Alberto's or Verga's
words. Whatever the case, it is not easy to think that they represent
the ultimate expression of cynicism, as the context seems to suggest.
After supposedly achieving by means of Alberto's speech both a key
psychological transition and the framing up of a sharp contrast between the man's disillusionment and Adele's still fresh and somewhat dreamy personality, Verga has the woman immediately decide
to marry the allegedly tired and spent Alberto in the hope of sharing
with him her own confidence in life. This decision, however, is
much too abrupt.

As soon as they are married, they move to their villa near Pistoia.
Alberto behaves like an ideal husband, until they return to Florence, where they see Princess Velleda Metelliani, who, being jealous of their happiness, seduces Alberto. Adele is willing to forgive
and forget, but Alberto feels trapped and leaves home again. Adele
becomes gravely ill; he manages to be back only in time to see her
die. As a result, Alberto plunges into the depths of despair, realizing, too late, that Adele's love could have brought him true life. The
novel closes with the melodramatic line: "And a gunshot was
heard."

Evidently this Alberto is not the hardened cynic Verga would
have us believe. He is a complex but very sensitive man; he has
made many mistakes, but he seems to be aware of them, even if he
has great difficulty verbalizing this awareness. His great attachment
to Adele, and then his leaving her after yielding to Velleda's wiles,
as if to accept some sort of expiatory isolation, may be considered a
proof of the complexity of his awareness. The same must be said of
his compulsion to follow her in death. Such a man may be called
excessively proud, but not cynical.

Verga wrote this novel in order to prove a thesis, but then he let
his character get out of hand. Whether he realized it or not, the
theme of the second part of *Eros* is how life repeats itself and how a

man of forty-five can still fall prey to the images of his youth. If Verga had been able to concentrate on this theme of the continuing tyranny of the impressions of youth in a man's life, he could have created a very significant book. Even the carefully planned premise—Alberto's growing up without family, alone with his unrealistic yearnings for women and love—would have fit perfectly. But Verga did not look deeply into his character, and thus he put him in contradiction with himself. The other possible way to make the novel more plausible would have been to abandon the thesis and end the story with the first part.

The most coherently drawn characters of *Eros* are Adele and Velleda. The former is a girl whose strength lies in her sentiments, and whose reason for living is the man she loves. Velleda is her counterpart: proud, egotistical, hungry for the satisfaction she can derive from her power over others. The sympathy of the reader, as well as of the author, goes to Adele. However, we must admit that both women are quite undeveloped and somewhat static; neither of them appears to grow up and mature. At the end they are exactly the same persons as at the beginning. Velleda is the real force behind the action of the novel. If one is truly cynical, that one is she. In her irrepressible drive for self-assertion, she becomes a dark, evil goddess, injurious to both Adele and Alberto—even though her direct appearances are few and far between. Again Verga, while concentrating on Alberto, did not realize that Velleda brought an entirely new emphasis to the novel. If, on the other hand, we should judge her as a stereotyped, conventional, wicked woman, the situation would not change.

Among the minor characters, Countess Orlandi is a mixture of Narcisa *(Una peccatrice)* and Nata *(Tigre reale)*, but with the corrective features of Eva. She is passionate and sensual, but also knows the rules of life and of society. When Alberto declares himself ready to retire to a secret place where they can live by their love, she realistically retorts that circumstances do not allow her to follow him. Directly connected with her is one Colonel Morteni. Some time after his encounter with Count Orlandi, Alberto discovers that the colonel is the countess's new lover; he seeks him out and challenges him to a duel. But Morteni convinces him that there is absolutely no reason to go that far; the two have a drink and take leave of each other on good terms. The few pages devoted to this episode are bitterly humorous and parodistic. Later Verga would write of the deadly serious Sicilian duels—those dictated by deep elemental passions and occurring in the tragic privacy and in the silence of the cactus hedges. The Marteni-Alberto rivalry is indeed absurdly inane when compared to what Turiddu and Alfio will experience in "Cavalleria rusticana."

Uncle Bartolomeo constitutes a new character for young Verga. An uncomplicated man, he takes care of his farms and has well-defined aims in life. Intent on making money, he does so with great success, and when he dies he leaves behind a very substantial patrimony. He may be considered a Mastro-don Gesualdo in embryonic form. He is also the only *Eros* character to suggest one of Verga's great future protagonists. The Alberto type will never be taken up again; Adele may remind us a little of Mena in *I Malavoglia*, yet she is a much paler figure; and if we might be inclined to see in Velleda a preview of the Duchess of Leyra in the third novel of the *I Vinti* (The Doomed) series, we must also admit that, since Verga wrote only a very small section of that novel, any such comparison would be totally arbitrary.

The fact that *Eros* contains a great deal of social polemics indicates that Verga is annoyed with the very world he is trying to portray. These polemics are one of the roots of the failure of the novel; for no one can persistently state how deeply he loathes a social milieu and at the same time do a dispassionate job of presenting it. Prince Metelliani personifies this irritation of Verga's with the pretentious emptiness of the aristocrats. He is not a character, but simply a pretext.

Of considerable interest is the language of *Eros*. The dialogue often rings true and spontaneous. Verga makes a great effort to adhere to a certain environmental reality to such an extent that once he even peruses an actual piece of news reported by the local newspapers. His characters speak idiomatic Florentine, even if not always very accurately. Thus language and environment are beginning to coincide far more consistently than in his previous works. Verga also tries to insert the words of the characters in the narrative stream, thereby making use of what was later to be called "free indirect speech," a germinal form of interior monologue. "It was she who had passed on to her that rag of a husband when she didn't know what to do with him any longer" (p. 181), writes Verga, relating Velleda's resentment about Adele's married happiness. Those words are not the narrator's but the character's; in fact, if we substitute "she" with "I" we have Velleda's own speech.

Most critics summarily dismissed *Eros* as a work of very little significance. In 1903 Benedetto Croce decided that it was "emptier than the previous novels" and that it revealed the hand of a tired writer.[20] As in many other cases, Croce's opinion was taken at face value and repeated by subsequent scholars, even by the most serious and reliable ones. Unquestioned acceptance of whatever the celebrated Neopolitan philosopher and critic had written about a book or an author became one of the unfortunate practices of Italian scholarship for nearly half a century. Thus Luigi Russo disposes of *Eros* by stating that it appears to have been written by a man suspended between the desire to finish it and the regret of having begun it.[21] Even such a normally acute critic as Giacomo Debenedetti reproduces the Croce/Russo opinion.[22] Carmelo Musumarra asserts that Verga's psychological introspection has greatly improved, but then he agrees with the previous judgments.[23] More recently, Aurelio Navarria has declared *Eros* a significant novel, but has not been able to explain satisfactorily why.[24] Probably the source of such negative appraisals must be found on the one hand in the general inability to separate the first from the second part, and on the other in not perceiving either the complexity or the more personal style of the novel. Riccardo Scrivano, however, in an article of a few years ago, has made a valid attempt to place *Eros* in the proper perspective,[25] even though he has not supported his remarks with a detailed analysis. This analysis is nevertheless offered by Roberto Bigazzi, with a series of observations that tend to emphasize the importance of the novel in Verga's growth and development.[26] And finally G. P. Marchi stresses the merits of *Eros* with the intent of proving that it represents the "most mature" of Verga's early narratives.[27] In my opinion, it cannot be denied that as a work of art *Eros* fails; but it is one of those failures that carry a great deal of weight in an author's career. We must go, therefore, further than Marchi and recognize that of all of Verga's early novels, it is the one to offer a definite indication that the time when the still-young writer will be able to create a masterpiece must not be very far off.

VII   *"Nedda"*

This novelette was published in the middle of 1874, probably in June, by Brigola of Milan. Conceivably, Verga interrupted *Eros* in the spring of that year and completed it in a very short time. It is the first of his short stories, a genre in which he was to become one of

the masters. The young Verga aimed at novels, at book-length narratives; now he begins to seek more concentration.

The subject matter and the characters' environment are quite
new. Verga turns his attention to the lowest social levels in Sicily
and to characters who are passionate and honest, but who also have
great difficulty in winning their battle for survival. The theme of the
story will not, then, spring from his personal involvement in, and
direct observation of, high society, but from the memories of his
own childhood and adolescence—when he had seen the hard life of
the peasants, had witnessed the silent dramas of their extreme poverty, and had perceived the elemental force of their passions. After
spending years with people who had everything and were actually
dying of boredom, he must have longed for those uncomplicated,
but much more meaningful, human emotions he had once known.

The theories of the *Scapigliati*, coupled with the naturalistic
trends coming from beyond the Alps, and the emerging principles of
Verismo, certainly were for Verga a stimulus toward a new approach
to fiction—especially if we consider that to him being true to life
(*verismo*) implied, among other things, abandoning bourgeois
characters in favor of the poor in the faraway provinces. Strangely
enough, the latter were thought to be more true to life than the
former. But for the writers it was a means to renounce stereotyped
situations and characters, and to renew themselves by courageously
accepting a different perspective.

Of course, to present the poor and their hard lives as faithfully as
possible was nothing new. In Manzoni's masterpiece, to mention
the most famous example, the protagonists were two North-Italian
peasants engaged in escaping the capricious persecutions of the
all-powerful local lords and in building a life of their own; Ippolito
Nievo had written of peasants in his shorter narratives. And in the
early 1870's Zola was applying his pseudoscientific beliefs to the
inhabitants of the Parisian slums.

Verga might have been influenced by contemporary trends rather
than by past examples, but we must believe that the main impulse
to try his hand at a more congenial character came from within him.
He had already given signs of leaning in this direction. In the preface to *Eva* he had announced that the story was "true . . . without
rhetoric and free of hypocrisy," although he had not been able to
keep his promise. In *Eros* he had taken up a subject that forced him
to engage in constant polemics against his own protagonist. Still in

Eros he had written a statement that must be placed in the framework of his own artistic history: "The whole science of life consists in simplifying human passions and in reducing them to their natural proportions" (p. 165). It is an odd statement, for "simplifying" and "reducing to natural proportions" may, and may not, be synonymous. Yet its spirit reflects what Verga was to do later: to present human feelings as they are, in their natural essence, and not as they appear from behind the impenetrable mask of the infinitely distorting social hypocrisy.

Thus we should not wonder if at this moment, with so many factors conspiring to push Verga in a new direction, Nedda sprang up from his memory and forced herself onto his pages. The extra-long opening paragraph of the novelette is intended to be a preamble, and as such it repeats the modes and the methods of Verga's earliest works. It reflects his state of perplexity regarding both the environment and the characters. Apparently the new heroine and her Sicilian countryside exert a profound attraction on him, yet he still feels partly bound to a bourgeois world and to its psychological adventures. As he is pulled in two directions at once, he decides to solve his problem by resorting to an explanation—to himself, of course, much more than to his readers. But this lack of confidence which produces the preamble will survive throughout the story, thereby weakening and damaging what could otherwise have been a masterpiece. That opening paragraph, which is by far the worst part of "Nedda," is written in the style of the most conventional prose of the day; it is not only incredibly flat, but it also overflows with exasperating commonplaces, such as "the fireplace . . ." that was seemingly "created only to frame the gentlest and most serene domestic sentiments," or "just like the rays of the moon are meant to kiss blond hair" (p. 13).[28] One of young Verga's favorite terms is there too: "voluptuous," which, together with the corresponding noun ("voluptuousness") and adverb ("voluptuously"), is one of the most frequent, and least meaningful, words of his early novels. In "Nedda" it will appear during the course of the story, even where it will insert a badly strident note. Thus the familiar word will tend to put Nedda in the same company with Narcisa (*Una peccatrice*) and Eva, where she cannot possibly belong. Stylistically, Verga is far less daring than in the choice of his protagonist.

The preamble rambles along for many interminable lines. Finally, we are informed that the author sometimes leaves his body in his

armchair before the fireplace and lets his mind wander great dis-
tances. It is precisely during one such moment that the nearby
crackling flame evokes another flame, in the immense fireplace of
the Pino farmhouse, where on one rainy day the olive-picking girls
have gathered to dry their clothes. There he hears someone calling
Nedda; the girl appears; and the story begins. This clumsy and
roundabout way of getting to the point demonstrates decisively that
Verga not only intends to suggest that he is extracting Nedda and
her story from his own Sicilian past, but also that he is somewhat
uncertain of himself, and therefore unable to begin *in medias res*.

In itself the plot of "Nedda" is remarkably uncomplicated, as will
be the case with all the stories of Verga's maturity. Nedda, a poor
Sicilian girl whose mother is gravely ill, goes to work as an olive
picker to earn her bread and a little additional money to buy
medicine. Whether she works or not, and thus whether or not she
makes her wages, depends on the whims of the weather. She accepts the inevitability of this law with stoic resignation. Her
mother's condition worsens; so Nedda has to return home to see her
die. The day after the funeral Nedda must go back to the Pino farm.
Meanwhile, she has met Janu, a young man who makes his living by
pruning olive trees. The two find comfort in each other and soon
Nedda is pregnant. Janu decides to go to work some distance away
for the purpose of earning the money he needs to get married. He
catches malaria, the fever causes him to fall from the high branch of
a tree, and soon he is dead. Nedda remains alone. Nobody gives her
a job. The townspeople look down on her because she is "disgraced." Her uncle Giovanni is the only one to help her with some
food; but it is not enough. She gives birth to a little girl, who slowly
dies of malnutrition. The last words of the story are spoken by the
protagonist: "Oh blessed you who are dead! . . . Oh blessed you,
Virgin Mary, who have taken my child, not to let her suffer what I
have suffered!" (p. 38).

A plot of this sort contains all the ingredients of the works of
Verga's maturity. The characters, hopelessly trapped in extreme
poverty, are destroyed by events, without being able to do anything
to change their destiny. Their psychology has repeatedly been called the psychology of the doomed, which consists not so much in an
inevitable defeat as in an innate resignation to the blows of life and
in the unshakable belief that things have always been so and will
never change. Verga places a great emphasis on the background and

social environment of his protagonist. Poverty is viewed not only as a deterministic element, but as the most decisive of forces. Even Nedda's physical appearance has been shaped by poverty. Her destiny is the same as that of all the other poor, and no one can conquer it. The man she loves tries to earn some extra money, but as a result he dies, and in turn her little girl dies too. Love and the possibility of having a family are indeed luxuries the poor cannot afford. The power of the economic factor, which was already present in *Una peccatrice* and in *Eva*, is now explored anew, and far more convincingly. The writer has transplanted it into its own natural ground.

Verga's attitude throughout the story is one of unwavering compassion for the creature "crouched on the lowest step of the human ladder" (p. 16). He manages to bring out her feelings more successfully than he had done with any other character, but he also allows his personal compassion to lead him into frequent moralizing. He constantly calls Nedda "poor girl" and constantly attacks the people around her for being inhuman. Such direct intrusions and comments constitute one of the shortcomings of the story. The true artist does not judge; he represents. The judgment may spontaneously emerge from the page, but it is never expressed directly. Verga is not as yet capable of portraying the world of the poor in its stark inevitability by letting the facts speak in their own voice. This inability is reflected also in his style, which continues to be marred by frequent lapses.

But we cannot forget that in "Nedda" there are also some great passages, terse and concise, where every word is necessary and irreplaceable. Those belong to the Verga of the future. One of them is the really impressive page in which Nedda and Janu enjoy their brief hour of love. In it, natural background, characters' personality, and language are welded together in near-perfect unity. Nedda and Janu live an instinctive, supremely innocent moment, and Verga offers it to us effortlessly and without embellishments. Their dialogue is equally instinctive, swift, and in perfect harmony with their rustic psychology. That page demonstrates, among other things, that Verga has discovered the essentiality of dialogue. The declaration of love springs from their emotions as naturally as life itself. Verga has a donkey bray and has Janu take advantage of this event for the purpose of explaining to Nedda that donkeys bray because they are in love. Thus Verga has found a way to present

external elements as inseparable from the emotional world of his
characters—and has done so with incredible spontaneity. The 1874
anonymous reviewer of the *Nuova Antologia* objected to that bray-
ing, and went on to say that if writers should proceed in that direction, soon the readers would have to close their eyes and hold their
noses.[29] Instead, it generates one of the high points of the story, and
at the same time it foreshadows many great passages of "Jeli il
pastore" (Ieli), of "La lupa" (The She-wolf), as well as of other
masterpieces, including *I Malavoglia*, where the Sicilian countryside and the sea are conceived only as integral parts of the characters' everyday lives. Whenever Verga is truly an artist, external
elements invariably become interiorized.

In 1880, while reviewing that remarkable series of Sicilian tales,
Vita dei campi (Life in the Fields), Luigi Capuana said: "Perhaps
when he wrote 'Nedda,' Verga did not realize that he had found a
new lode in the still unexploited mine of the Italian novel."[30]
Capuana was referring to the contents of the story and to the
cherished *verismo* theories he thought Verga had applied, but subsequent critics read his sentence as an intimation that "Nedda" not
only was a masterwork, but marked the abrupt beginning of its
author's greatness. Later Croce added that the novelette had introduced "a fresh note" in Verga's literary production.[31] This was a
cryptic statement which needed much explanation. But once again
Crocean critics took it as a highly authoritative judgment and tried
to prove its validity by subjecting it to all kinds of variations. They
were generally misled by the background and the setting of the
story. Their reasoning went more or less as follows: Verga's great
works are almost without exception set in the poorest sections of
Sicily, and since "Nedda" has the same setting and the same type of
characters, it must also be great. Probably they did not realize that it
is impossible for a writer to mature overnight and suddenly write a
masterpiece. The results of an independent personal reading were,
on the other hand, offered by Thomas G. Bergin in 1931. He made
excellent observations, but on the whole he too limited himself to
contents and gave the impression of being excessively enthusias-
tic.[32] Some recent scholars have been more circumspect, and after
studying "Nedda" anew they have managed to place it in the general
context of Verga's artistic history.[33]

"Nedda" cannot be considered either Verga's first mature work or
a sample of what he would do in the years ahead. It carries the seeds

of a great story, but great it is not. While it affords us a glimpse into his future achievements, it also bears witness to Verga's groping past. It is the somewhat clumsy product of a man who has finally discovered a compatible world, but does not yet understand it fully. That the dialogues are often so natural and spontaneous is partly due to the novelty of that world. Verga cannot escape a style and a language that are more sober, more concrete, more fitting to the innate reticence of his Sicilian peasants, and, therefore, free of sophistication and falsification. But when he presents his characters and their background directly, and speaks and describes on his own, his prose reveals the same old blemishes.

Had Verga omitted the rambling preamble, cancelled all the moralistic comments and all the strident and diluting expressions, he might have created a superior piece. In 1897 he included "Nedda" in a new edition of *Vita dei campi*. On that occasion he polished and further improved many of those Sicilian tales, but did not touch "Nedda," which badly needed revision.[34] Thus he left unchanged the main document of his slow growth. "Nedda" must have had considerable significance for him even personally from the very moment he completed it. In fact, not long after he began another Sicilian story. It was in September 1875 that he wrote to his publisher, Emilio Treves: "Soon I'll send you *Padron 'Ntoni*, a novelette about fishermen."[35] That novelette was to be written again and again for the next six years, until it turned into one of the great novels of the century, *I Malavoglia*. "Nedda" can indeed be viewed as the distant, though irresolute, beginning on the road to the masterpiece.

VIII Primavera ed altri racconti

After "Nedda" and after completing *Eros*, while painfully trying to write *Padron 'Ntoni*, Verga's pen kept meandering in other directions. *Primavera ed altri racconti* (Springtime and Other Tales)—published in 1876 and later reprinted as merely *Novelle* (Stories)— can be regarded at best a series of diversionary pieces, interspersed in the difficult and most challenging stages of a far more compelling work.

The setting of the title story is Milan, and its social environment is rather unsophisticated. A would-be musical composer and a milliner try to forget their respective disappointments by having an affair. Soon he is oppressed by lack of money; and even his lovemaking

tends to become a burden, the repetition of the same gestures. He
is offered a good-paying job in an American tavern and takes it. The
lovers' last two days are full of memories and melancholy. The girl
knows that there is no other choice, and accepts her loneliness with
complete resignation. She subconsciously understands that love is a
luxury and cannot really exist without money. The only good passage of the story portrays the parting at the station, when the girl
passively follows her man's every footstep until the final good-bye is
lost in the impersonal noise of the crowd. Otherwise, the general
tone is saccharine, obviously addressed to a certain segment of the
reading public. However, Verga does seem to make a consistent
effort to harmonize his language with the environment, by trying to
spice his pages with a bit of Milanese. It is the result of his determination to be "realistic." Apparently, he has not discovered as yet
that true realism does not consist in photographic reproduction of
external details, but in their recreation in terms of the inner life of
the characters.

"Primavera" calls to mind Henri Murger's *Scènes de la vie
bohème*, which from 1847 on generated a series of popular narratives and plays until, by the end of the century, it found its highest
interpretation in Puccini's *La Bohème*. Yet "Primavera" should most
appropriately be placed in the context of the Milanese *Scapigliatura*. It is, as Gaetano Mariani contends, both a general presentation
of the *scapigliato* way of life and Verga's first portrayal of two
wretched young people in the cold, foggy Northern Italian city—the
man personifying the typical young artist rejected by local groups,
and the girl reflecting a common literary figure of the time, in the
tradition of Giulio Carcano and Iginio Tarchetti.[36] But it must be
added that in Verga's previous works there were predecessors, like
Enrico Lanti and Eva, that encouraged such a choice of characters.
Later on, he will take up again some of the themes, as well as the
peculiar city atmosphere, of "Primavera," and will give them new
life in the Milanese sketches of *Per le vie* (Through the Streets), his
best non-Sicilian short stories, published in 1883.

The novelette, "Le storie del castello di Trezza" (The Ghosts of
the Trezza Castle), is a far more ambitious work. In general terms, it
belongs with all the Romantic tales in which the unhappy spirits of
the dead are heard howling in the wind. In our specific case, it
marks the point when Verga begins to look to Sicilian folklore as one
of the possible components of his writing.

In the ruins of the old castle, Verga says, people can still hear laments and see ghosts on stormy nights. Two lovers, Luciano and Matilde, are now visiting the ruins with Matilde's husband. After having dinner in the old tower, Luciano tells the story of a baron who used to live in the castle, and who finally one night killed his unfaithful wife; like a ghost, she had been coming to steal food from the pantry to sustain her sick lover in the grotto below the castle. At the end of the tale, the three visitors decide to return home—but they must cross a very narrow and dangerous bridge some five hundred feet above the rocks. The husband goes first, followed by the two lovers, furtively holding hands. When they reach the center, Matilde's husband, who obviously knows what has been going on, abruptly turns his head and calls to her. She is startled so badly that she loses her footing and falls into the ravine, pulling Luciano along with her. People still say they hear laments around the castle and see ghosts on stormy nights.

The plot is clearly organized in two separate parts, the first of which is chronologically the second. Luciano and Matilde are face-less and distant, while the Baron and his unfaithful wife, who should merely function as a suggestive parallelism, move to the foreground and totally overshadow their counterparts. In addition, Verga constantly tries to interweave reality and legend by means of interruptions and flashbacks for the sole purpose of keeping the reader in suspense. But as a result, the story is badly structured and its tone is quite uneven. Here and there, however, a sentence or a phrase bears the mark of a truly vigorous writer. There is even an extremely suggestive passage. At a critical point, just before committing adultery, the baron's wife goes to the window and looks at the sea: "The fishermen, scattered on the shore, or clustered before their huts, were chattering about fishing tuna and salting anchovies . . ." (p. 117). It is impossible to read this sentence without thinking of *I Malavoglia*. One wonders if it came to Verga's pen only because he was in the process of writing *Padron 'Ntoni*, "a novelette about fishermen."

The other pieces collected in *Primavera ed altri racconti* are much less significant. "La coda del diavolo" (The Tricks of Life) was written "for those people who spend their time searching for the reason why everything human is logical on one side and absurd on the other" (p. 149), and it is riddled with philosophical inconsistencies and overly dramatic banalities. It is difficult to understand why

Verga wrote it. The theme of "X" (The Mark X), chronologically the first piece of the séries, is the egocentric search for self-gratification, which excludes all feelings and all possibility of communion. The setting in Milan, as Olga Ragusa observes, has remained only potential: "it is neither fully developed setting nor unmistakable atmosphere and mood."[37] The thin and conventional plot and the some what unstructured prose are typical of the early Verga. It is conceivable that the conclusion was originally intended for the closing pages of *Tigre reale*—and that later Verga expunged it from the novel, but found it so irresistible as to feel compelled to write an entire new story in order to utilize it. "Certi argomenti" (A Certain Kind of Reasoning) hinges on the strange pride of the idle, which is motivated by a compulsive desire to assert one's own ego. Frightening risks are incurred for no resulting gain whatsoever. The story is disappointing in that it is intended to be ironic, but ends up by being merely cynical.

We must conclude that *Primavera ed altri racconti* does not contribute much to the history of its author; with the conceivable exception of the title piece, no story seems to carry much significance. It was probably published for the sole purpose of having another book in print, and for the revenue it would bring. This motivation must not be considered irreverent, however, for to Verga money was as important as it was to his own Mastro-don Gesualdos.

Verga's concentration on shorter works at this point may be viewed as an indication of his growing need for conciseness of style, as well as for unity and coherence in the enucleation of the inner world of his characters. The fact that he published two volumes of such compositions in sequence—*Primavera ed altri racconti* and *Vita dei campi*—can serve to point up the maturing author's developing awareness of the infinite possibilities inherent in his chosen material (the representation of human passions "without rhetoric and free of hypocrisy"), and of the ineluctable necessity for bringing such potential under control.

CHAPTER 2

Maturity: Vita dei campi *and the New Style and Language*

O F the stories in *Primavera ed altri racconti,* "La coda del diavolo" was possibly the last to be written. It also turned out to be the one to close an era in Verga's personal history. In 1877 his sister died, and in 1878 his mother followed her to the grave. These events plunged him into periods of depression and of extended meditation on human destiny, and undoubtedly they brought his vision of life into sharper focus. Meanwhile, he was forced to spend a great deal of time in Sicily, and his Milanese friends began to intimate that he had given up writing altogether.[1]

However, the crisis Verga was undergoing during those years was determined not only by grief, but by having tired of a certain world and of certain characters, precisely as a result of a more strenuous and more realistic approach to life. In 1879, while still laboring at *Padron 'Ntoni,* he wrote to Capuana that the new work "would be in immense contrast with the turbulent and unending passions of big cities, with their fictitious desires and demands. . . ."[2] He was referring to a radically different human content, but he was also implicitly speaking of a style as sober and as intense as the lives of the characters. He had become convinced that style and subject matter are one and the same thing, for the subject matter comes to life and gathers vigor only inside the words chosen. This belief had been slowly maturing in him, when he suddenly became conscious of it. Many years later he told the following story:

I had published some of my first novels. They were selling. I was planning others. One day I happened to lay my hands on a logbook. It was a rather ungrammatical and asyntactical manuscript, in which the captain succinctly related certain difficulties his ship had faced—in a sailor's style; without a word more than necessary; briefly. It impressed me. I re-read it. It was what I had been unconsciously looking for . . . A flood of light.[3]

41

We do not know when this incident took place; we do not even know whether it is true or not. What we know, however, is that the logbook cannot be held responsible for Verga's stirring and unmistakable style. The anecdote very probably indicates a point of consciousness—the moment when Verga clearly realized that to be himself he had to conquer a personal realm of words, at once simple and rich in underlying tension.

I *"Fantasticheria"* (Images)

After years of trial and error on the pages of *Padron 'Ntoni*, Verga began to use the interludes and the empty spaces born of his own dissatisfaction to experiment with his stylistic concepts in a series of short narratives that were to rank among the best produced in Europe during the second half of the last century.

Rather than a story, "Fantasticheria" is a series of images and meditations. It represents both an introduction to Verga's mature work and a statement of transition. The author had visited Aci-Trezza, a poor fishermen's village on the Eastern coast of Sicily, together with an elegant city lady. She had chatted with some of the fishermen and had shown passing interest in their families. Then she had left, saying: "I don't understand how anyone can live here all his life" (p. 146). To live in such a place all one's life, Verga now comments, is much easier than it looks. All it takes is not to have a comfortable income. Besides, notwithstanding all hardships, these people may even have fuller lives than the rich of the cities. They, Verga admits, have chosen an oyster's life, and like oysters each stubbornly clings to his rock. Yet they are at least as respectable as those who find them ridiculous. The members of a family stick together and work together for the common good as if guided by some inviolable sacred principles—the principles of the *religione della famiglia* (p. 151), the "religion of the family hearth." Their wisdom is the product of the experience of an untold number of generations, and their human feelings are sound and natural, not spoiled by complicated and fictitious desires. Actually, their way of life may even be quite desirable.

Obviously, Verga's lady personifies the world of high society, and stands in marked contrast with the provincial and unvarnished society of his youth. He had known that world during nearly fifteen years in the cities that had fascinated him with their glitter. But now he needs to reconquer the roots of life, the unmarred nudity of passions, and this he can accomplish only by turning to the poor of his Sicily.

Since the lady left Aci-Trezza, many things have happened to the family that especially attracted her attention. The old man had to die alone in the village hospital, his son was devoured by the sea, one of his grandsons was killed in the war, the other ended up in prison, and a granddaughter lost herself in the city. This is the plot of *I Malavoglia* in a nutshell. It is followed by a statement which also gives away one of the main points of the novel:

When one of those poor and simple people—either the weakest or the least prudent, or, perhaps the most selfish—decided to break away from his family, because he was driven either by desire for the unknown or by yearning for an easier life or by curiosity to see the world; that world, which is such a voracious monster, devoured both him and his close relatives (pp. 151–52).

Verga calls this "a drama of some interest" and promises to recount it. It is, in fact, the drama of young 'Ntoni Malavoglia, who drifts away from his family, and is devoured by the world. But now Verga seems to think that those who cling to their rock like oysters should not try to escape, for, if they do so, they violate the very principles governing their existence; they betray the *religione della famiglia,* and, consequently, meet their own destruction. In the novel, on the other hand, he will at least theoretically recognize that this is precisely how social and economic improvement can be achieved and, while many must fall by the wayside, their sufferings are a necessary component of the march of progress.

In "Fantasticheria" Verga plays two worlds against each other. His sympathy goes to the unspoiled freshness of the second. Yet it is not Romantic sympathy for the "picturesque" lives of the poor, but it springs from a profound source. He had mingled with those people during his young years, and either consciously or unconsciously he had continued to contrast them with those he had met in the cities. In *Eros* he had stated that the real science of life consists in reducing human passions "to their natural proportions." Now he can finally go back to his people with full understanding, to rediscover those "natural proportions" precisely among the fishermen of Aci-Trezza and in the "immense" fields of the Plain of Catania.

II *"L'amante di Gramigna."* Verismo. *Style and language*

If in its entirety "Fantasticheria" must be viewed as a statement of transition and a conscious return to the Sicily of his youth, "L'amante di Gramigna" (Gramigna's Mistress) is first a declaration of narrative principles, and then a practical example of them. The two narratives complement each other perfectly and can be considered the best and most comprehensive preface to the writer's mature work—the first bringing to the fore a psychological preference, and the second representing an effort to carry out what we may vaguely label as the ideal of the logbook.

"L'amante di Gramigna" first appeared as "L'amante di Raia" in the February 1880 issue of *Rivista minima*, a periodical edited by Salvatore Farina. It acquired its present title in September of the same year, when it became part of *Vita dei campi.* The story is introduced by a letter to the editor, which is of extraordinary significance not so much for what it explicitly says as for what it suggests. The opening paragraph reads as follows:

Here is not a story but the sketch of a story. It will at least have the merit of being very short and of being factual—a human document, as they say nowadays. . . . I shall repeat it to you as I picked it up along the paths in the countryside, with nearly the same simple and picturesque words characterizing popular narration, and you will certainly prefer to find yourself face to face with the naked and unadulterated fact, rather than having to look for it between the lines of the book, through the lens of the writer (p. 203).

"Factual" and "human document" are further developed by Verga when he mentions the science of "human passions" and the perfect novel of the future: "its every part will be so complete that the creative process will remain a mystery . . . its manner and its reason for existing so necessary that the hand of the artist will remain absolutely invisible . . . ; it will have the imprint of an actual happening; the work of art will seem to have made itself" (p. 204). All this has a familiar ring, for it repeats some of the fundamental tenets of French naturalism as they were assimilated by the writers of the Italian *verismo* school. Consequently, at this juncture I must digress enough to present as briefly as possible the substance of that literary school and the far-reaching effect it had on Verga's career.

Verismo (being "true to life") was the name given to revitalized realism during the second half of the nineteenth century by a group of Italian writers in opposition to the fantasies of late Romanticism. While Verga is generally considered the main representative of that school, many others directly or indirectly accepted its principles. Among them we must include Luigi Capuana, a good novelist and a still better critic; Federico De Roberto; Emilio De Marchi; Renato Fucini. Even young D'Annuzio was *verista;* and so was Matilde Serao. The trend continued well into the twentieth century with Grazia Deledda, Federico Tozzi, and Bruno Cicognani. *Verismo* lies at the very foundation of all subsequent Italian literature. Even Pirandello, who focused on so many problems of unusual complexity, was rooted in *verismo;* and so was Svevo, who wrote one of the European masterpieces of our century. The same must be said of Giovanni Pascoli, who initiated the new Italian poetry by throwing open the doors of the inexhaustible storehouse of spoken, everyday language.

Historically and generally, realism may be viewed as either a philosophical doctrine or as a literary method. In both cases it has a fairly long history. As a philosophical doctrine, it gained its greatest ascendancy during the eighteenth-century, mainly in England and France, and in the nineteenth-century, mainly in Germany. As a literary method, it dates back to the Greeks of the Alexandrine era, and to the Latins of the silver period—notably Petronius Arbiter— but it flourished in the works of Boccaccio, and later in many writers of the Italian Renaissance. It is difficult, for instance, to imagine anyone more deliberately realistic than Pietro Aretino.

During the middle of the nineteenth-century realism became rather popular in various European countries, especially in France and in Italy, where—in spite of the Romantic movement (or perhaps because of it)—the continuing tradition of set literary rules had become a stifling trap. In Italy Manzoni might be defined as a realist, but his followers and imitators stressed his so-called moral ideals. The Milanese *scapigliati,* who had some influence on Verga and Capuana, chose "realistic" principles that actually intermingled with the weaker manifestations of late Romantic psychology.

But the man most responsible for promoting a new approach to literature in Italy was Francesco De Sanctis. His profound knowledge of the culture of the past and his familiarity with the literature of the present enabled him to offer personal interpretations on a wide variety of topics. In September 1868 De Sanctis published in the influential *Nuova Antologia* an article entitled "Petrarca e la critica francese" (later reprinted as an introduction to his celebrated *Saggio critico sul Petrarca*), which reads like a profession of faith in the principles of realism. After painting a rather dismal picture of contemporary writing, he came out with a statement perfectly epitomizing the substance of the essay: "What is there to be done now? . . . To replace the 'ideal' with the 'real.'" We may contend that in De Sanctis's mind this statement must be connected with Vico, whom he defines "concrete" and "the true father of the new art," and with a "rejuvenated" Faust, the symbol of science . . . searching for truth through the study of nature.[4] But it is unquestionable that in realism (De Sanctis adopted the newly coined term, *verismo*, only late in life), he saw the rebirth of literature.

If De Sanctis's enthusiasm for realism will surprise those who associate his name merely with the rigorous critical principles by which the value of literary works must be judged only on their own merits, it can be understood and justified in the framework of an era when the need for renewal was deep-seated and widely felt. But to the young writers grouped in Milan the encouragement to try different avenues came from France, where Comte's positivistic philosophy was integrated with the teachings of Taine and with the sociological applications of Darwin's recent scientific discoveries. These influences rapidly led to naturalism, with Balzac and particularly Flaubert (who had lent credibility to the theory of "impersonality") being looked to as the forerunners of the movement. And soon Emile Zola was the one to become not only the master, but the personification, of naturalism.

The bridge between traditional realism and the explicitly proclaimed naturalism of Zola and his followers can be found in *Germinie Lacerteux*, published in 1864 by the Goncourt brothers. If Zola's *Thérèse Raquin*, published in 1867 and reprinted in 1868 with an important preface by the author, became the mother of all subsequent naturalistic novels, the Goncourt work certainly influenced Zola and helped him to discover his own inclinations. In the 1870's many writers looked to Zola as the initiator of a new literature. In Italy what De Sanctis was saying and the *scapigliati* were unconsciously looking for, was thought to have finally been accomplished by the dynamic young French writer.

According to the principles of naturalism, the writer must study his human subjects with the scientific objectivity of a physiologist or a physician, and must present them with equal detachment. It was, in fact, from a treatise on experimental medicine by Claude Bernard that Zola said he had derived his theories on the novel.[5] Human reality must further be viewed from the standpoint of its own irreversible deterministic laws of heredity and environment. In practice this is done by seeking out the people of the city slums, the corrupt and the degenerate, by observing how they act and react, and by ascertaining how their degeneracy passes from generation to generation. Being the result of this observation, the novel almost writes itself through the characters' actions and reactions.

Italian *veristi* believed in some of the principles of naturalism, but, with the exception of the theory of impersonality, or detachment, they did not make any special attempt to apply them. They did not seek out the corrupt and the degenerate, and on the whole they rejected the deterministic law of heredity. They did not even call themselves naturalists, but simply "neo-realists" (which may be the accurate translation of the term *veristi*). They looked for the reality of human passions in the simple, and eternal, interplay between man's actions and man's aspirations. They did not go to the slums in search of characters, but to the faraway provinces, where they thought man to be more genuine, not yet psychologically complicated, or deformed, by the "civilization" of the cities. They stressed the inner world of their people by bringing to light their strong impulses for life and their innate morality. Of course, the fact that Italy offered so many different regional environments made their task easier. Yet we cannot forget that the *veristi* kept finding their characters in the regions of their youth. This would have made it impossible for them to look at those characters with the clinical eye of the scientist, even if they had chosen to adhere to the letter of naturalism. Their acceptance of the theory of impersonality, on the other hand, helped them to keep in check any possible intrusion of sentimentality. Thus we may conclude that *verismo* can be defined as the offspring of the marriage between preexisting realism and naturalism. As with all offspring, it soon showed its independence from the parents, even if its personality continued to be marked by some of the most conspicuous characteristics of both.

Ever since his early years Verga had studied his men and women carefully and had tried to portray them with objectivity. In a letter to Felice Cameroni, dated July 18, 1878, he asserted: "I have always attempted to be true to life, without being either a realist or an idealist or a Romantic or anything else, and if I erred and did not succeed, too bad for me, but such was always my intention—in *Eva*, in *Eros*, in *Tigre reale*."[6] Thus he took himself out of contemporary discussions on naturalism. But if it is true that he did not adopt Zola's "scientific" method, it is difficult to see how he could have written "Nedda," or how he could have applied the deterministic principles of cause and effect in *Eros*, or especially how he could have written the introduction to "L'amante di Gramigna," without being aware of the emerging new European literary trends. Verga regularly brushed aside classifications and labels. He considered schools of secondary significance and insisted on art: "There is room for all trends and for all writers," he said, "and everyone can produce a work of art. What counts is that the work of art comes into being."[7] But this does not exclude his acquaintance with naturalism, his direct collaboration in the development of *verismo*, and all the benefits of self-discovery he derived from it.

The main spokesman for *verismo*, Luigi Capuana, expressed in theory what Verga managed to achieve in practice. In the preface to *Profumo* (Scent, 1890)—looking back to his young years when he had not yet understood the principles of the new literature—he stated that then he, as well as many others, had not realized that "the true ideal lies in reality itself, as it happens and as it changes." This thought is amazingly similar to what De Sanctis had written in 1868, in the preface to his *Saggio critico sul Petrarca*. And thus we are brought back to the beginning of our digression.

Verga's introduction to "L'amante di Gramigna" must then be read in the literary climate of *verismo*, as it developed in Italy during the 1870's. Most of its terminology derives from French naturalism, but it is absorbed into an independent context, as demonstrated by the phrases referring to language—"as I picked it up along the paths in the countryside, with the simple and picturesque words characterizing popular narration." This declaration springs not only from Verga's own intention to write straightforward and naked prose similar to the prose of the logbook, but also from the generally accepted belief in popular literature, or folklore—conceived by many as a fresh and powerful manifestation of human creativity and, therefore, as an unparalleled model, and an inexhaustible source, for writers.[8] Such a belief became a logical component of the *verismo* theories. A number of authors explored the lower levels of the social ladder in the conviction that the tales and the language uncoverable there bore the imprint of unsurpassed originality. The case of Verga is, of course, much more complex. But he, too, drew from local tales and characters. We know, for instance, that "L'amante di Gramigna" and "La lupa" (The She-wolf) are based on stories of real people and were inspired by Capuana. Later on, when Capuana himself wanted to pay "L'amante di Gramigna" his highest tribute, he said that Verga had recreated the events with an artistic power rivalling popular narration.[9]

With Verga, however, we should not be misled by his statements into thinking that he intended to transcribe directly what he heard. The dense spontaneity of a text cannot be improvised, nor can it be found in someone else's schematic recounting of an event. Verga wrote and rewrote until he had found a satisfactory mode of expression. Of "L'amante di Gramigna," for instance, even without taking into account all the probably discarded versions, we have no less than three different printed readings—and all three are totally divergent, in both presentation and narrative details, from the "real" story as it was later told by Capuana. "Popular narration" represents, then, nothing more than the name Verga is giving to his own ideal of narrative prose. Through it he can attain "the naked and unadulterated fact"; he can fulfill, in other words, the illusion of complete objectivity, in accordance with the principles of *verismo*.

As implied in his note to Cameroni, Verga was conscious that in most cases his previous works were somewhat approximate and ineffectual because they had been written in a style lacking firmness and power. His phraseology had been drawn from the average bourgeois language and was thus made up of expressions that had been worn out and rendered nearly meaningless by continuous usage. The characters clothed in that language were equally superficial, often without even a semblance of really profound life. Thus, when he speaks of the sea captain's log, as well as when he says that he is relating the story with the simple words characterizing popular narration, on the one hand he admits the shortcomings of his previous writings and on the other he declares his determination to abandon empty literary molds in favor of fresh and unadorned expressive patterns. It is in this context that we must place a statement Verga made to Ugo Ojetti in 1894, when he said that it is not by studying the dictionary, but "by listening and listening that we learn how to write."[10] He knew that every writer has to create for himself a language perfectly suitable to the world of his characters.

He looked for this language in the environment and in the lives of the characters themselves. However, as he could not find what he was seeking, he immediately discovered that he had to invent a language, which was to be ideally their natural medium—not an expressive optical illusion, but a profoundly alive, and natural, instrument of communication, even though it was different from the external reality of their speech. His fishermen and his peasants did not know standard Italian at all. Had he translated them into the shallow bourgeois idiom of the time, he would have destroyed the intensity of their feelings. And since it would have been impossible to clothe them in Sicilian dialect, he was indeed forced to create a language in which they could fully place their personal implications. It was a most fortunate coincidence.

For his purpose Verga adopted a great many local expressive patterns and grafted them onto the old trunk of standard Italian. With very few exceptions, every word of the mature Verga can be found in a common Italian dictionary. Not always standard Italian, however, are certain cadences and certain rhythms which evoke an environment and a way of life belonging only to Sicilians. The syntax is extremely simple, spoken—its structure consisting chiefly of a seemingly unending sequence of coordinate clauses linked together by the conjunction *e* (and).

Once the expressive choices were made, the same effort toward objectivity led Verga to a technical discovery of fundamental importance. He began to narrate in the words of his characters. Until then, even the most poignant stories carried in every sentence the personal imprint of the author. His own stories, on the other hand, sound as if they were mainly related by an invisible popular narrator who belongs to the same social milieu as the protagonists and who has witnessed the events. While this method justifies the original language mixture, it also makes it almost natural to introduce the thoughts and the comments of the characters into the narrative stream. When we read Verga, we are often under the impression that the characters are narrating themselves, in their own peculiar terminology—and that, therefore, they are painting their own portraits. This has caused some critics to speak of "dialogued narration,"[11] and of "free indirect speech."[12] In reality, we are confronted with an embryonic form of what years later will be defined as interior monologue, which Verga attained simply through his compelling desire to be "true to life." He declared that all he had tried to do was to put himself "under his characters' skins . . . to see with their eyes and to speak in their words."[13] He did not realize that in the process he had begun to employ the techniques of modern narrative prose—at least to some extent.

With "L'amante di Gramigna" Verga began to strive for the greatest economy of words and for maximum condensation. Not only did he refrain from any direct intrusion into his text, but eliminated everything that could be suggested between the lines. Above all, he avoided traditional descriptive passages. The very fact that he was narrating with the words of his people forced him to be unceasingly intent upon their individual reactions. As a result, he could mention external elements only when those people mentioned them—that is to say, when they found them relevant to their everyday lives. Thus description per se was automatically eliminated.

On July 10, 1879, Francesco De Sanctis proclaimed: "The motto of serious [literary] art must be this: let us not talk, but let us make things talk."[14] It was exactly what Verga was beginning to do in a much bigger way than the great critic could have anticipated. Verga's highest and most consistent accomplishment in this sense is represented, as we shall see, by the entire novel *I Malavoglia*. But for perfection and originality, many of his Sicilian short stories should not be placed on a much lower level.

In "L'amante di Gramigna" Verga focuses on a girl, Peppa, who falls in love with a bandit without having ever seen him. She leaves her home and her fiancé, follows the bandit as he is hunted by the police, is wounded by a gunshot, and finally, when he is caught, she becomes a cleaning woman in the barracks adjoining the jail, and is filled with admiration for the *carabinieri*, who have proved even stronger than her man.

On the surface the theme is very simple, for it is concerned with some quite basic psychological principles. But, as with all artistic products, what makes the story outstanding is the way in which the theme is treated, and how it finds concrete realization in the style. Verga immediately creates an air of wonder and places the bandit in the center like a legendary figure, alone against a thousand. In comparison, those who are chasing him ("all those gentlemen of the police department") look ridiculously small. Throughout the opening paragraph we immediately sense a deliberately popular, somewhat aliterary tone. The constant movement and activity are obtained with the simplest expressive means. Incidental comments, obviously repeating remarks by the observers, are inserted into the narrative stream with extraordinary ease (e.g., "a name as cursed as the grass that bears it" [p. 204]—*gramigna* is the Italian for crabgrass). The same tendency to tell the story in the words of the villagers is evident in the alogical use of mixed metaphors which are often intended to produce an impression of awe ("sgattaiolava come un lupo" [slunk like a wolf, p. 205]: the Italian "sgattaiolava" is applicable only to a cat). The syntax is based on an elementary sequence of quick, identically structured phrases. In its appearance this prose is very unsophisticated, yet it communicates with immediacy and without distractions.

In that opening paragraph Verga singles out one factor of Gramigna's "desperate flight": his "burning with thirst," in the immense burnt plain. For Peppa, who has fallen in love with his exploits ("that one, that one was a man!" p. 206), that thirst grows to the point of becoming all-exclusive, of turning into the very essence of the bandit's difficult life. Through a direct psychological transference the girl too experiences the same thirst, every morning, and needs to satisfy it. It is, of course, the symbol and the counterpart of another thirst, of another deep, personal need. Thus she leaves her home and goes looking for him. When she finds him, he does not want her, but then he sends her to get a flask of water. She is shot at, and when she returns she is like him, "bleeding, her clothes torn" (p. 207). Now her process of identification with her man is complete. She will follow Gramigna everywhere, suffering the same hunger and running away from the same police bullets. When he is caught, she is caught with him. Then she goes home and hides in the kitchen, "just like a wild animal" (p. 208). After her mother's death, she looks for the jail where Gramigna was supposed to be. But he has been moved to a safer place. Yet she decides to remain there and be a servant to the *carabinieri*, whose strength she admires.

In a story of only a few pages Verga manages to create a highly poetic character. His stylistic compression, rather than preventing, helps him to evoke some profound human associations. A few words, or the repetition of a key phrase, are enough to bring to the surface even what lies hidden in the subconscious. With "L'amante di Gramigna" Verga has definitely opted for certain characters and has conquered a prose born of their inner world. Although they are the poor and the oppressed, these characters are full of existential intensity, and although they cannot rebel against a social structure that has from time immemorial assigned them to their present condition, they do indeed live by their desires and aspirations, and above all by their dignity and sense of morality. Verga has them

express the ordinary/extraordinary events in their lives with a vehemently personal language, through which they stand out and
tower. Thus he turns the poor and the oppressed into the heroes of
his time.

III *"La lupa"* (*The She-wolf*)

Published for the first time in the same month as "L'amante di
Gramigna" (February 1880), it picks up again the theme of female
sexuality and turns it into a fierce and inescapable call, like destiny
itself. The protagonist, Pina, may be defined as a mixture of Nata
(*Tigre reale*) and Velleda *(Eros)* transferred to the sunburnt fields of
Sicily. But her behavior is more convincing than that of either of
them, and her personality is far more powerful than both combined.
Like the opening page of "L'amante di Gramigna," the beginning of
"La lupa" reproduces the townfolk's awestruck conversation. They
use all the means at their disposal to overcome the effects of her
presence in the community; they even resort to exorcising gestures;
but to no avail. Thus the figure of the She-wolf immediately stands
out as the living embodiment of a natural force no one can possibly
resist; it becomes greater than legend. Far more powerful than
Gramigna, the She-wolf can reap victims at will.

That beginning again proves how Verga can move freely along the
lines of popular narration. Its components do not follow a preestab-
lished logical order, but are juxtaposed in an irrational, or impres-
sionistic, manner. We are informed, for instance, that the people
called her "the She-wolf," but suddenly she is metamorphosed into
a "wild bitch"—the two definitions being obviously felt as equiva-
lents. According to the women in the town, she *first* "sucked the
blood of their sons and husbands" and *then* she "pulled them behind
her skirt" (p. 139), while in a logical sequence the reverse would be
more plausible. The mention of the altar of Saint Agrippina quickly
brings about the remark that she never went to church and the still
more important reference to Father Angiolino. This is associative
prose, intended to produce the greatest impact with the concluding
detail: "Father Angiolino of Saint Mary of Jesus, a true servant of
God, had lost his soul on account of her" (*ibid.*). That such a man,
whose immunity from evil is warranted by supernatural forces,
should become her defenseless victim, does indeed prove the She-
wolf's immeasurable might. Now we know that she *is* the inescapability of the flesh, even stronger than the supernatural. Verga has

been able to say all this, and more, in only a few lines. He has found words that truly create. Now there is no question that he is quite a different writer from the author of *Una peccatrice* and *Tigre reale.*

After devouring all kinds of men, this woman falls in love with Nanni, who is young and strong, and within reach. She falls in the fullest sense of the word, "feeling the flesh afire beneath her clothes" *(ibid.).* At harvest time she works furiously in the fields just to be next to him. Nanni wonders why, until one evening she tells him: "It's you I want. You who are beautiful as the sun and sweet as honey. I want you!" (p. 140). Nanni answers that he does not want her, but her daughter Maricchia, who is young. Ready to do anything for him, the She-wolf promptly agrees. Maricchia refuses, until she realizes that she must obey her mother.

The passage in which Pina forces her daughter to marry Nanni is a masterpiece of condensation: "Nanni was all greasy and filthy with oil and fermented olives, and Maricchia didn't want him at any price. But her mother grabbed her by the hair before the fireplace, muttering between her teeth: 'If you don't take him, I'll kill you!' " (p. 140). In these few lines the scene shifts abruptly. The first sentence has the characters standing by the olive press in the barn and the second presents Pina and Maricchia at home. The shift is accomplished with a single "but," which assumes a heavy burden of implications. It is an example of how Verga eliminates all that can be understood between the lines and focuses on what is essential to reveal the inner movements of his characters.

Pina may have sensed that, by having Nanni in her own house as Maricchia's husband, she would find some sort of vicarious gratification and that, consequently, her passion would subside. Instead it flares up still more fiercely, as Nanni fully understands when she looks at him. He tries to repel her silent call by resorting—he too—to religious symbols and gestures. The implicit struggle between religion and the flesh continues throughout the story. But we already know which one of the two will emerge the winner.

One summer afternoon, while the Sicilian countryside lies motionless under a scorching sun and no one would dare go walking about, Pina is overwhelmed by the fire in her flesh:

"In those hours between nones and vespers when no good woman goes roving about," Pina was the only living soul seen wandering in the countryside. . . .

"Wake up!" said the She-wolf to Nanni, who was sleeping in the ditch along the dusty hedge, his head in his arms (p. 141).

Sicilian folklore tells us that "the hours between nones and vespers"—the early afternoon—are under the spell of malignant spirits. Here they become the hours of the She-wolf. We see her tower in the deserted fields, everything around her engulfed in the immobility of expectation. The countryside, as well as the gruelling sun, is now, more than the counterpart, the very projection of her flesh afire.

Nanni stretches out his groping hands. But later, in the clutches of guilt, he sobs in despair: "No, no good woman goes roving about in the hours between nones and vespers!" (p. 141). This is how Verga isolates a seemingly casual proverbial saying and gives it his own imprint by enclosing in it the deepest feelings of a character. He will soon use this phrase once more, with Nanni waiting impatiently for the She-wolf "in the hours between nones and vespers." "The hours between nones and vespers" has thus grown to express Nanni's irreversible destiny. And the She-wolf is it.

In my comments upon "L'amante di Gramigna" I intimated that Verga was beginning to discover the lyrical value of repetition. By restating a key word or a central phrase, he could bring to the surface what lay hidden in the subconscious of his characters. Stylistically, "La lupa" is still far more clearly embedded in this technique. The proverbial "between nones and vespers" is an example of it. As in this case, the expressions Verga repeats are always extremely common—so much so that at first the reader does not perceive their weight. It is a poetic device, somewhat similar to the *leitmotiv* in music. By means of recurrent words and images, poets can achieve deeply suggestive results.

The story continues by bringing Maricchia briefly into the limelight. She is grieved by the affair, and, more practical than Nanni, she does not resort to religious gestures, but asks the *carabinieri* sergeant for help. As he is questioned, Nanni acknowledges his inability to ignore the afternoon call of the She-wolf. Soon after he is kicked in the chest by a mule and is at the point of death. But he recovers.

Here the invisible narrator indulges in a spontaneous commentary, which, like the choral parts of the Greek tragedies, forebodes

the impending doom: "And it would have been better for him to die
that day . . ." (p. 143). Nanni tries every avenue to escape the
She-wolf's spell and his own guilt. But nothing seems to help. Finally, he chooses the ultimate remedy: " 'Listen!' he said to her.
'Don't come to the threshing floor again; if you do, I swear to God,
I'll kill you' " (ibid.). The She-wolf can have but one answer: "Kill
me, I don't care; I can't stand it without you" (ibid.). After this, an
extraordinary paragraph concludes the story:

As he saw her from the distance, in the green wheat fields, Nanni stopped
hoeing the vineyard, and went to pull the ax from the elm. The She-wolf
saw him come, pale and wild-eyed, the ax glistening in the sun, but she did
not fall back a single step, did not lower her eyes; she continued toward
him, her hands laden with red poppies, her black eyes devouring him.
    "Ah! damn your soul!" stammered Nanni (p. 143).

It is the tragic catharsis, the only means for her to be freed from her
subjugation to the flesh, and the only way for Nanni to recover his
real self. The She-wolf, again towering in the middle of the fields,
walks toward death with the countenance of a queen. This is our last
impression of her. We do not even see her fall under the ax; we
simply notice that in her final appearance she carries bundles of red
poppies—the double symbol of her passion and of the blood she is
about to shed because of it.
    "La lupa" is the most compressed of the stories of Vita dei campi.
In 1896 Verga translated it into a two-act tragedy. He diluted and
weakened the original pages, as we shall see in the chapter on his
theatrical works. But the central concept remained unchanged.
Some time later, in a letter to his Swiss-French translator, Edouard
Rod, he defined it as the tragedy "of the She-wolf's blind, animal-
like, but almost fateful passion."[15]

IV   "Cavalleria rusticana"

Originally an episode of an early draft of I Malavoglia,[16] "Cavalleria rusticana" was published as an independent piece in March
1880. Today we find it difficult to imagine that it could be part of the
novel, even though there may be some coincidental similarities
between young 'Ntoni Malavoglia and Turiddu, and even though in
both works one of the main characters is named Alfio. Due mainly to
Mascagni's opera, the plot is generally well known. Here suffice it to

say that each character's actions are determined by the same motivation and that, again as in Greek tragedies, each one unwittingly does
all he can to collaborate with destiny in working out his own destruction.

In reference to the stories of *Vita dei campi*, Luigi Russo spoke of
the "lyrical upsurge of the primitives"[17]—"those primitives" who, at
a certain time, presumably force themselves on the writer and on
his pages. This formula implies that Verga grasped with extraordinary immediacy some of the major drives of man at their most
natural level. But if we wish to consider Verga's Sicilians as primitive, we must also admit that they are deeply social human beings
and have an instinctive feeling for social order—which rests, among
other things, on the respect for the rights of others, in defeat as well
as in victory. If those rights have been violated, the victim is not
only justified, but expected, to regain his privileges and thereby
restore an equilibrium. Thus Turiddu must try to get Lola back;
Santa must report Lola to Alfio, because she feels that now Alfio
belongs to her; and Alfio must punish Turiddu for having taken his
wife. Only with the ultimate disappearance of Turiddu will Lola
belong to her husband, and thereby the social balance will be reestablished. Turiddu himself is aware of this; in fact, in his last speech
he says to his rival: "I swear to God I know I have done wrong, and
I'd let you kill me . . ." (p. 137). In this type of society there is a
great sense of justice—a justice that must be administered without
hesitation by the very people who have been offended. Such a rule
is never questioned, for it is conceived as the codification of some
fundamental human needs.

Stylistically, "Cavalleria rusticana" is not as consistently original
as "La lupa," but in the most convincing parts it continues to employ
the techniques of that story. In some cases it moves even further. In
"La lupa" a triple repetition turns a proverbial expression into the
symbolic synopsis of the characters' irresistible impulses. In
"Cavalleria" the same device interiorizes an external, at first seemingly insignificant detail—to the point of making it the mirror of a
basic psychological attitude. In the opening lines of the story, for
example, we learn that Turiddu was wearing his red military cap,
"that looked like the one worn by the fortuneteller" (p. 131). As the
story progresses the cap, or rather its tassel, reflects the embarrass-
ed disappointment of the young man's masculinity, since the
woman he loves, Lola, has become engaged to Alfio ("he walked

behind the girl, swaying, while the tassel of his cap danced here and
there on his shoulders," p. 132). Still later that tassel ripens to the
full maturity of the rich and vivid symbol of Santa's personal yearning: "the tassel of the *bersagliere*'s cap had tickled her heart and was
forever dancing before her eyes" (p. 134). Thus Verga has been able
to present a common occurrence (a girl falling in love) in highly
original and poetic terms.

But it is in the mastery of the free indirect speech that "Cavalleria
rusticana" reveals the writer's greatest progress. For the first time
Verga can naturally and effortlessly insert the words and thoughts of
his people in the narrative texture. Here is how he gives Turiddu's
reaction to the news that the man from Licodia, Alfio, had taken
Lola away from him: "As soon as Turiddu found out, damn it! he was
going to tear that Licodian's guts from his belly, he was!—but he did
nothing of the kind" (p. 131). The first part of this passage reproduces Turiddu's own angry words, including even the emphatic
repetition of the main verb, as normal with this character throughout the story. If we rewrite it in the present tense ("Damn it! I am
going . . . etc.") we will have Turiddu's direct speech. This is a
most immediate, I should say, prerational method of narrating. Now
that free indirect speech has long since grown into the interior
monologue, and the interior monologue into the stream of consciousness—so much so that both have apparently exhausted their
potentialities for some time, and writers have been looking for new
narrative techniques—my observations may be of little consequence. But in 1880 Verga's method was quite original and contributed greatly to the rich tenseness of his pages. It also
foreshadowed, though embryonically, some of the most conspicuous
prose of our century.

Here it may be appropriate to point out that if "Cavalleria rusticana" became the most popular of its author's short stories, it was
not due to its literary qualities. In 1883 Verga rewrote it as a one-act
tragedy, which was an instant success mainly because, in an age of
saccharine bourgeois theater, it shocked the audiences into the
realism of violent passions; but, as we shall again see, the tragedy
remains stylistically inferior to the story. Then, in 1890, G. Targioni-Tozzetti and G. Menasci reworked its plot into a libretto that
young Mascagni set to music. It is self-evident that the opera belongs to the history of a different medium and, obviously, cannot be
examined with the criteria of literary art.

V *"Jeli il pastore" (Ieli)*

Strikingly different from "La lupa" and "Cavalleria rusticana," this is a novelette in which Verga explores the possibility of a new narrative rhythm and the relationship between chronological and psychological time. He closely watches the development of a peasant boy who is left entirely to himself, for whom life is an unending series of discoveries, and who grows up to be a man with the same feelings and the same sense of justice as those who have been guided and indoctrinated by a social group.

Deeply attached to the horses he tends, Ieli feels they are his only friends, the only creatures with which he can communicate. Like a young colt himself, he gambols with them, runs in the fields, and fully shares in the innocence of nature. Occasionally, during the summer months, he also experiences the companionship of a rich boy, Don Alfonso, who brings him delicacies and tells him about what he is learning at school the rest of the year. To Ieli school represents an impenetrable, mysterious world, open only to the privileged; yet he never resents being excluded. One day something new comes into his life, a little girl by the name of Mara; he begins to spend a great deal of time with her, hardly ever speaking a word. However, after his father dies, Ieli feels alone and defenseless. He begins to wander with his herd and does not see Mara for a long time. When he returns, she has grown into a big and pretty girl. Coincidentally, she is preparing for a move with her family to a distant town. As she disappears in the valley Ieli cries out: "Mara! Oh! Mara!" (p. 164), and knows that now he is truly alone. Those last, inarticulate sounds close a marvelous idyllic period; they are the growing boy's call after his disappearing childhood. Had Verga finished his story with them, he still would have created a little masterpiece.

With that first part, he intended, among other things, to examine the past of a man who, having grown up in a friendly, primitive environment, is naïvely optimistic and, consequently, is slow in understanding the everpresent treachery of life. Thus the fabric of "Jeli il pastore" comes to rest on the dialectical conflict between such naïve optimism and the realities of the human condition. We may even venture to state that in it Verga is tacitly arguing against one of the most popular among the late Romantic views of life. The happiness of childhood, he seems to say, can neither last nor can it be recaptured; in fact, it should not be. Man must grow up to be alert, well-prepared and well-armed to defend himself from both circumstances and the ruthless selfishness of the adult world, or he will be destroyed.

At the beginning of the second part we learn that Mara has gotten engaged and does not even remember Ieli, while he, in his solitude, keeps thinking about her. One year, early in the morning on St. John's Day, while he takes the colts to the fair—and he is lost in thought over Mara—there emerges at the top of the grade a carriage full of cracking of whips and jingling of bells. The colts scatter in a flash. He regroups them, but instantly notices that his favorite, Stellato, has fallen into a ravine and has broken his back. Ieli sits by Stellato until the factor comes to shoot the colt and to fire him.

This is a turning point in the story. Through an event over which he has no control whatever, Ieli's dreamy optimism gets the first serious blow. It will soon be followed by others, which will come on the crest of a series of variations on the double theme of his recurring sense of dejection and of the carefree, festive mood of the people around. He goes to the fair and wanders in the crowd with the hope of seeing a friendly face: Indeed he meets Mara's father, who will eventually help him find a job as a shepherd. With Mara he goes to watch the fireworks, but the girl shows very little interest in him, for she is all excited about her fiancé, Massaro Neri's son. When Ieli sees him kiss Mara, "the whole fiesta, which he had enjoyed until then, changed to poison" (p. 174). Thus he, in one fateful day, has lost his job and has found and lost his girl. Yet he cannot quite accept such harsh realities.

Now a shepherd at Salonia, he works hard to learn his new trade. Meanwhile, he hears that Massaro Neri's son has jilted Mara because she was carrying on with Don Alfonso, but quickly rationalizes this out of his mind; in fact, he can vividly remember Don Alfonso as the pleasant boy-companion who would not do wrong to anyone. Mara comes to a little farm her father owns in the area and encourages Ieli to ask her to marry him. The wedding is celebrated without wasting time for preparations.

Ieli has to spend his days at Salonia tending his sheep, thus seeing his wife only twice a month. He asks her to go with him, but she refuses. Once he returns home unexpectedly in the middle of the night and is kept waiting outside in the rain. When he is let in, he notices that the back door is open, but he does not give it much thought. Even if his friends at Salonia tell him that Mara is carrying on with Don Alfonso, he cannot believe them, for his resurgent childhood is again and again chasing present realities away. But one day the farm owner invites all his friends for a picnic dinner. While the rich young men are dancing with the girls, Ieli is shearing his sheep. At a certain moment Don Alfonso calls Mara, who has insisted on coming to the picnic. Ieli tells her not to dance, but she goes anyway, and as he sees her languidly abandon herself in Don Alfonso's arms, he immediately understands. He gets up, his shears in his hands, and cuts the man's throat with a single stroke. Later, when the police are taking him to court, Ieli keeps saying: "What? . . . I shouldn't even have killed him? . . . But he had taken my Mara! . . ." (p. 186).

The entire story gravitates toward this final paragraph. Ieli's "understanding" is the ultimate defeat of his optimistic disposition, while his violent reaction is the only one which seems both natural and respectable. In fact, his very words indicate that killing Don Alfonso was indeed the least he could do under the circumstances, and that being arrested because of it is indeed incomprehensible—like being arrested for having done one's duty.

As already noted, in "Jeli il pastore" Verga pursues also a narrative exploration of the interrelationship between chronological and psychological time, and opts for the latter. He almost totally disregards the actual sequence of time periods and dwells exclusively on events with a lasting emotional impact. There is no way to tell, for example, how many years elapse between the beginning and the center of the story. Ieli was a happy child, and suddenly he is an adult facing the difficulties of life. The transition is merely hinted at by the incidental phrase: "so much water had passed and passed under the little bridge" (p. 165), as if all that had left an indelible mark on the child had already been told and the rest represented nothing more than the repetition of obvious thoughts and of obvious gestures. Interestingly, we do not feel we miss any details. If anything, we are even under the impression that the narrative pace is slower, more leisurely and more diffuse, than in the other stories. And in spite of the chronological gaps, we know that the three parts constitute an indivisible unity, all imbued with the same, deep-flowing lyricism.

Through memory man instinctively selects from his past a related event and fully relives it in a special dimension—as belonging exclusively to the present. At that moment, time in a chronological sense does not exist. We may object that in life there is always a sequence, a before and an after; however, the perception of this sequence is the product of our rational faculties, which compel us to see events in a so-called logical order, or, rather, to translate the subconscious into the conscious. When by association we relive past experiences, we actually make them contemporary. Then only psychological time does really exist, and it is unidimensional: present. In "Jeli il pastore" Verga has to reconcile the protagonist's continual withdrawal into this dimension of past-present with the possibility of his becoming fully aware of what is happening around him. To do so, he has decided to tell the story on two different but synchronously amalgamated planes, without ever losing sight of either one of them. This explains why he can convincingly present an Ieli who so easily dismisses any unpleasant information and who, on the other hand, finally grasps reality and quickly yields to a homicidal impulse.

But even remaining on a more common level, we like to point out how, through his character's perception of time, Verga happens to achieve some significant narrative innovations. The Monday after the wedding, Ieli has to return to the distant pastures but cannot quite make up his mind to leave his bride. He lingers about, and finally he says to Mara: "You should come to Salonia too!" But she answers laughing "that she wasn't born to be a shepherdess." These words produce the following paragraph.

In fact, Mara wasn't born to be a shepherdess, and she wasn't used to the north wind of January when your hands stiffen on the staff and your fingernails seem to be falling out, and to the furious rainstorms when the water goes through to your bones, and to the suffocating dust of the roads when the sheep move along under the scorching sun, and to the hard bed on the ground and to the moldy bread, and to the long silent and solitary days when in the burnt countryside you could see nothing but a rare sun-blackened peasant driving his little donkey silently ahead of him on the white, endless road. At least Ieli knew that Mara was warm under the covers, or spinning by the fire with her neighbors, or was enjoying the sun on the balcony, while he was coming back from the pastures tired and thirsty, or drenched with rain, or when the wind drove the snow into his hut and put out the fire of sumac wood (p. 180–81).

Here every single expression is born of Ieli's personal experience and of his tender feelings for Mara. Past and present are fused into a simultaneous emotional condition. Ieli is an adult, but his considerate attitude toward Mara stems from the days of his childhood and summarizes his entire personal history. Thus Verga, by presenting interwoven levels of time from the viewpoint of his character's emotions, expands the free indirect speech and brings it closer to the modern interior monologue.

Since the prose of "Jeli il pastore" is often intentionally allusive, we may be tempted to see in the above passage a subterranean vein of bitter irony, in the sense that Mara wanted to stay home simply because she was waiting for Don Alfonso. But such is not the case. Verga concentrates on Ieli's feelings and succeeds in creating a lyrical synthesis of unusual intensity. As to irony, he never uses it directly, but lets it spring from the words of his characters or from those of his invisible narrator, as happens on the page through which we learn that Ieli is a cuckold, while he is unaware of "his disgrace" (p. 182). In the general structure of the story, however, that page too has a precise function: to complete the portrait of the protagonist, both by stressing his innate naïveté and by telling us how people around him react to it.

VI "*Rosso Malpelo*"

To many critics the best of the *Vita dei campi* selections, "Rosso Malpelo" tells of a boy who has to be mean and mischievous only to protect himself, and whose behavior is firmly grounded in a peculiar philosophy of his own. Meanwhile the experimentation with the treatment of time is carried further than ever. If in "Jeli il pastore" Verga had eliminated many transitions, the reader could still perceive some sort of chronological sequence. Now even this barely perceptible sequence seems to have been abolished, so that we are left with the impression that many events take place simultaneously. Reading "Rosso Malpelo" is like watching a canvas being slowly uncovered, piece by piece, until we can finally see it in its entirety.

The nickname in the title, "Redhaired" (Rosso) "Evil-haired" (Malpelo), condenses a common superstitious association whereby a certain behavior is the natural result of a person's looks—and vice versa. This is strikingly stated in the first two lines, which also reflect all the irrationality that had produced such a belief: "He was called Malpelo because he had red hair; and he had red hair because he was a mean and a bad boy who promised to turn into a first rate scoundrel" (p. 187).

Malpelo works in a sand quarry; everybody calls him names, kicks him in the pants, and throws rocks at him. They say they keep him out of charity, because his father, Misciu, died there, one Saturday night, while on a contract job and the big sand pillar caved in. Malpelo has never forgotten that moment, nor has he forgotten the wickedness of the people who did nothing to rescue his father. Now he hates everybody at the quarry, but cannot revenge himself because they are stronger than he. He has become convinced that men are bad and life itself is evil. The only way to survive is to attack. But fortunate are the dead, for they do not suffer any longer.

He befriends Frog, a lame boy, and teaches him what he has learned. He hits him, then he says: "If you feel how blows hurt, you'll learn to give some yourself" (p. 191). He drives an old donkey that pants and sags under the burden, and he beats it saying: "The donkey must be beaten, because he can't beat us; if he could, he'd smash us under his hoofs . . ." (p. 192). When the donkey dies and the cart-driver carries the carcass away and throws it onto the lava beds, Malpelo reflects: "That's the way it is. Tools that can't be of use any longer are thrown away" (p. 197). Then, watching the dogs eating it, he says that now the donkey cannot feel the beatings, "but it would have been better for him if he'd never been born" (ibid.). He also tells Frog, who has TB, that it is better for him to die, and knows that this is true for himself, too. After Frog's death, Malpelo is really alone and almost looks for the moment when he too will disappear. One day the men at the quarry want to explore the possibility of connecting the tunnels with the great shaft toward the valley. No one wants to run the risk of being lost in the underground maze. Then they ask Malpelo, who will not be missed by anyone. Malpelo picks up his father's tools, and goes. He never returns. So ends the story which splendidly "celebrates the legend of a 'mean and bad boy' who has been transformed into a popular myth."[18] Malpelo is also the prototype of the victim of particular social attitudes, who has no escape except in actually becoming what everybody thinks he is.

Not very much seems to happen in the story, and yet we feel it overflow with momentous events, due to the fact that Verga does not narrate directly but through his protagonist's remarks. The flashback on Malpelo's father's death appears to function as the mover of the entire story. Not only all of Malpelo's observations on life and man, but even his final decision to go underground, spring from that same remote source. He is constantly fascinated by darkness and by tales about people lost in the quarry. He tells Frog stories about miners who were lost in the tunnels underground; one went in when he was young and came out with gray hair; another called in vain for help for years and years. " 'He alone hears his own cries!' he said, and at that thought . . . he started" (p. 198). When he picks up his tools and goes, he remembers this second case. Unconsciously, the voice of the miner crying out in the dark tunnels has for him turned into his father's voice. It is the theme of the relationship between Malpelo and his dead father that makes it possible for Verga to remain on a purely psychological level, while leaving actual chronology almost completely aside. Malpelo's stark and ruthless philosophy (similar to that of a primitive Machiavelli planted in a hostile world) also grows out of such a theme. By meditating on his father's death, he discovers the substance of the struggle for survival and can synthesize it into a personal concept of human existence.

The story as a whole is a magnificent piece of prose. It gives the full measure of Verga's narrative skills and originality of style. Here many of the features that we have discovered in the previous stories stand out with an even greater degree of maturity.

VII   *"Guerra di Santi" and "Pentolaccia"*

In contrast with the previous stories, generally ending in tragedy and death, "Guerra di Santi" (War between Saints) is woven on the lighter thread of comedy. The two sections of a small town are fighting on the assumption that the patron saint of one is much better than that of the other. A procession, blows among the parishioners, and the involvement of the mayor and other officials, constitute the tempestuous background of an otherwise ordinary romance.

Nino and Saridda are engaged to be married, but each belongs to a different district of town, and following the outbreak of "hostilities" each swears not to see the other as long as they live. Soon, however, there is a severe drought and cholera strikes. Saridda gets very ill and Rocco rushes to her bedside. She recovers, and the two are together again. But they are also the symbol and the counterpart of the entire town. In fact, all its inhabitants stop fighting and find a *modus vivendi*. Yet everyone remains convinced that his patron saint is the better one.

Tragedy returns with "Pentolaccia" (Stinkpot), whose protagonist,
vaguely resembling the adult Ieli, but far less developed as a character, is slow in realizing his peculiar family arrangement only because
he has been unsuspectedly living with it for a long time. "Pentolaccia" is written in exemplary prose.[19] The initial paragraph seems to
repeat the words of a villager in the midst of a circle of friends in the
public square or at the tavern table. After chatting about the strange
individuals he knows, he is finally getting to Stinkpot (a sarcastic
nickname containing what might be labelled as a lower-class sexual
image): "Now it's Stinkpot's turn; he is quite a character too, and
looks very good among all those animals at the fair. . . . He really
deserved that ugly name, for his pot was full every day . . . at the
expense of Don Liborio" (p. 221). Verga must have found it plausible to adopt this tone, as if introducing the last one of the "odd"
characters passing slowly through town. "Pentolaccia," in fact, concluded the first edition of *Vita dei campi*—a much more forcefully
coherent volume than it was to be in the subsequent printings,
when the original tightly knit unity was shattered by the addition of
an unrelated piece, "Il come, il quando ed il perché."

Stinkpot and Don Liborio, the local doctor, have been doing
everything on a fifty-fifty basis, sharing in landholdings and crops.
The doctor has understood that as part of the deal there was no
objection to his sharing Stinkpot's wife too, and has been doing so
freely. Everyone seems to be aware of this, except Stinkpot. But
one hot afternoon, while he is trying to get some rest behind a
hedge, he overhears his fellow workers remark that he has an easy
life only because he has engineered such a disgraceful family situation. He jumps to his feet, runs home, sees Don Liborio gingerly
leaving, and warns him that if he comes to his house again he will
kill him. The doctor cannot figure out why this man, of all people,
has suddenly become jealous, and quickly forgets the threat. The
following Saturday Stinkpot returns from the fields two hours earlier
than usual, picks up the door bolt, hides behind the wall, and—as
Don Liborio steps in—cracks his skull open with a single blow.

In "Pentolaccia" the jealousy theme is basically the same as in
"Cavalleria rusticana" and in "Jeli il pastore"; yet it appears to be
rushed and stifled. The effort to adopt the norms of popular narration has possibly been carried to the point where the protagonist
remains nebulous, without a clear-cut personality. It is true that,
like "Jeli il pastore," the story hinges on the idea that even the most

naïve, good-natured individual nurses deep feelings about his exclusive rights to his wife and cannot help eliminating the man who
takes her away from him. But Stinkpot's behavior is less persuasive
than Ieli's, precisely because the reader is not made aware of either
his background or of his sentimental attachment to the woman. The
entire story seems to be told from a point of view that is external to
the character, and thus it risks becoming abstract. Verga may have
fully succeeded in wearing his popular narrator's shoes, but he has
not been able to get under the skin of his protagonist.

Vita dei campi was printed in September 1880. At that time *I
Malavoglia* was well on its way to completion. As soon as the strenuous exercise in narrative patterns and the unfaltering originality of
style displayed in the short stories could be successfully applied to a
large variety of themes, the novel would rapidly attain its final form.

CHAPTER 3

Maturity: I Malavoglia

I *The Introduction*

DURING the years when Verga seemed to have given up writing altogether, and while he was searching for new characters, as well as for a suitable style, he became further acquainted with the works of Balzac and Zola. He also read Darwin and accepted the principle of the struggle for survival. His own deep-rooted conviction that only the achievement of financial security grants man the possibility of expanding and fulfilling all other needs, led him to identify the origins of individual and social progress precisely in the drive toward that achievement. By welding the visions of some other writers onto his own beliefs, he conceived a cycle of five novels, each one presenting and analyzing a successive stage in man's effort to gain financial well-being, and subsequently to assert it in an ever-widening social context. This design became clear to Verga in the early spring of 1878, when he wrote to his friend Salvatore Paola: "I am thinking of a work that I consider great and beautiful—a sort of phantasmagoria of the struggle for existence, extending from the rag-picker to the cabinet minister and to the artist, taking all forms—from ambition to greed—and lending itself to a thousand representations of the great human tragicomedy. It is a providential struggle which leads mankind to the conquest of truth by means of the most diverse desires, noble as well as base."[1]

The collective title of the five novels was to be *La marea* (The Tide), but two years later it was turned into *I Vinti* (The Doomed), a rather tragic definition many critics have applied to most of the characters born of Verga's maturity. The specific titles of the novels were already the same as those appearing in the definitive sketch of the project—with the exception of *Padron 'Ntoni*, soon replaced with *I Malavoglia* (commonly rendered into English as "The House

68

by the Medlar Tree"), and the *Duchessa di Gargantas,* who will turn
into *La Duchessa di Leyra.*

I Malavoglia was finally ready at the end of 1880 and was published in February 1881. It opens with a programmatic introduction,
which has often been neglected by the critics, and is instead extremely important—for in it the writer both explains his plan of
work and presents the artistic principles that must guide him during
its realization. He does so by bringing into sharper focus his remarks
to Salvatore Paola, and by interrelating them with some of the concepts he had expressed in the preface to "L'amante di Gramigna,"
thereby endowing them with greater depth and breadth.

This story is the sincere and dispassionate study of how the first anxious
desires for material well-being must probably originate and develop in the
humblest social conditions; and of the perturbations brought into a family,
who until then had been living in relative happiness, by the vague yearning
for the unknown, by the realization that they are not so well off, or that they
could be better off. . . . As the search for economic improvement by which
man is tormented grows and widens, it also tends to rise and to follow its
ascending movement into the various social classes. In *I Malavoglia* it is still
only the stuggle for material needs. Once these are satisfied, the search will
turn into greed for riches, and will be embodied in a middle-class character,
Mastro-don Gesualdo. . . . Later it will become aristocratic vanity in *La
Duchessa di Leyra,* and political ambition in *L'onorevole Scipioni.* Finally,
L'uomo di lusso will be possessed by all those compulsive desires, all those
vanities, all those ambitions; he will gather them within himself . . . and
will be consumed by them.

We might be tempted to assume that this theory—of proceeding
from the lowest to the highest social levels—was suggested to Verga
by Edmond de Goncourt, who, in his preface to *Les frères Zenganno,* states that a writer should first concentrate on the lowest
classes, for there men and women are more easily understandable
and analyzable, while the members of the bourgeoisie and aristocracy are difficult to present in their psychological complications.
Naturalism, according to Goncourt, could not be successful unless it
adopted such a pattern. But this derivation is unlikely. The preface
to *Les frères Zenganno* was written in 1879, and even if Verga had
read it by January 1881, he had found in it nothing more than a
corroboration of the ideas he had communicated to Salvatore Paola
early in 1878. It is far more possible that the common source for

both Verga and Goncourt is to be found in the widely held tenets of positivism. August Comte, in the second lesson of his *Cours de philosophie positive,* maintains that, when analyzing a set of phenomena, one should proceed from the simplest to the most complex ones. Thus, sociology, which devotes itself to the most complex of all phenomena, must naturally come last. Obviously, both Goncourt and Verga are in perfect harmony with the principles of positivism. But it must also be added that these theories might have been originally, if remotely, suggested by Darwin's studies on living species: nature, too, appears to have progressed from the simplest to the most complex forms. Finally, it is possible that Verga's plan to move from the lowest to the highest social classes simply reflected a notion that toward the end of the 1870's was generally accepted.

Mankind's fateful, strenuous, and feverish march toward progress—Verga continues in his introduction—appears to be grandiose in the outcome, if seen as a whole, from a distance. In its glory are lost the anxieties, the ambitions, the greed, the selfish compulsions that prompt it on an individual level. All the vices turn into virtues, for from a collective viewpoint the end-results justify every motivating impulse. This movement encompasses all human activities on all social levels; it is the great flood that sweeps everyone away. The observer, himself carried by the flood, may become interested in those who fall by the wayside, in the doomed who raise their arms in despair and bend their heads under the brutal steps of those who are hurrying on—the victors of today, who will be the doomed of tomorrow.

Such is Verga's vision of mankind's march toward financial security and progress. There are no winners, only losers. Before his eyes, Darwin's struggle for survival has turned first into a struggle for progress and then into a universally devastating effort to realize one's own greed and one's own ambitions.

The foregoing should not indicate that Verga conceived his novels as sociological dissertations, but rather that he gave himself an ideological platform on which to stand and from which to report the actions and reactions of the people he was observing. He devised a somewhat massive, and yet indefinite, frame merely because he initially felt that to give his work a purpose and a direction he could not lose sight of a comprehensive human landscape. He never lets his characters elaborate on the logic or nonlogic of their human condition, but simply lets them live it; he never lets them analyze their impulses, but simply lets them be driven by them.

But Verga's spectacle of all mankind marching on the road to progress, with so many of its members falling and being trampled upon, constitutes a vast vision that only a poet could have conceived and presented. Yet, when we meet his characters and discover that, while they may be pawns of intricate socio-historical forces, they are first of all struggling human beings driven by fundamental needs and irrepressible impulses, we experience a feeling of brotherhood. We, too, may be among those who are swept away by the raging flood. Verga himself ("the observer") was one of them. Of the five novels he had planned, only two were completed, and both can be read as independent masterpieces.

Very significant from another standpoint are Verga's statements regarding the style and language to be adopted for the five novels.

In those lower spheres [i.e., on the social level of *I Malavoglia*] the mechanism of passions is less complicated, and consequently it can be observed with more accuracy. All that is necessary is to leave the picture its own genuine and simple colors. . . . As the range of human actions broadens, the mechanism of passions becomes more complicated. . . . The language tends to be more individualized, and to be enriched with all the nuances and the ambiguities and sentiments. . . .

After the preface to "L'amante di Gramigna," these statements should sound fairly familiar. There Verga had declared that he was completely faithful to the actual events. Now he broadens this concept to extend it to the entire gamut of human activity—the basic approach, as well as the roots of his observations on style and language, being virtually the same. In "L'amante di Gramigna" he had spoken of "popular narration," implying a near transcription of the expressive patterns of both the protagonists and those who had witnessed the events. Now he tells us that the expressive levels will change with the social levels—according to the varying degrees of the characters' education, manners, and speech. Thus he will have to adopt an expressive medium that each time coincides with the inner world of his characters, so that he can let them narrate themselves—whether they are illiterate fishermen, shrewd landowners, members of the Palermo aristocracy, or Roman politicians. In the introduction to *I Malavoglia* Verga again presents his literary beliefs and his intentions, which he will later define as simply putting

himself "under [his] characters' skins," seeing with their eyes and
speaking in their words.[2]

The result of this plan was—as already indicated—that each time
Verga moved to a different social level, he had to invent a suitable
new language—a Herculean task indeed. He was magnificently successful in *I Malavoglia*, which requires a rather uniform language.
However, in *Mastro-don Gesualdo* he was confronted with the
much more difficult need of recreating at the same time the expressive medium of the bourgeoisie, of the wasted but still proud aristocracy, and of the common people. The magnitude of such an
undertaking may partly explain why the second novel of the series is
not as flawless as the first. He spent the rest of his life planning *La
Duchessa di Leyra* (The Duchess of Leyra), but he could never go
beyond the first chapters. The other two novels remained titles. If
his lofty expressive goal was, at least to some extent, responsible for
the success of his masterpieces, it ultimately made it impossible for
him to invent a language of social classes no longer appealing to him.

At the end of his introduction Verga speaks of the "observer"
standing aside from the universal struggle for progress, so that he
may study it dispassionately and render it "clearly and sharply, with
fitting colors, so as to represent reality as it actually was, or as it
should have been"—for "whoever observes such a spectacle is not
entitled to judge it." As in "L'amante di Gramigna," Verga insists on
objectivity, on the author having to remain distant and impersonal.
But at the same time, he seems to acknowledge that complete objectivity is indeed impossible, for a writer must constantly make
choices (certain characters, certain events, instead of others), thus
having to accept a personal involvement and the intrinsic expression
of a personal judgment. In fact, while maintaining that "whoever
observes such a spectacle is not entitled to judge it," he also states
that reality must be presented "as it actually was, or as it should
have been." That *as it should have been* constitutes a drastic departure from the preface to "L'amante di Gramigna" and from many of
the previous statements in the introduction to *I Malavoglia*. It tells
us that the hand of the artist restructures reality to the point of
turning it into his own creation.

In the March 14, 1879, letter to Capuana, referring to the composition of *Padron 'Ntoni (I Malavoglia)*, Verga writes: "I would
have liked to lose myself . . . among those fishermen, and catch
them alive, as they are. But maybe it will not be so bad to con-

template them from a distance, from the midst of a noisy city, such
as Milan or Florence. Don't you think that . . . we will never manage to be genuinely and effectively real except when we engage
ourselves in a work of intellectual reconstruction and replace our
eyes with our minds?"[3] This is another way of saying that a writer
presents reality "as it should have been," or rather as it emerges
from his own vision of it. Yet his efforts to achieve objectivity and
detachment were for Verga an important deterrent to personal intrusions into his narrative.

I *The Framework*

We know that in 1875 Verga had already completed a first draft of
a "novelette about fishermen," by the title of *Padron 'Ntoni*, but he
had decided not to have it printed—for, as he told his publisher, on
second reading he had found it "pale and watery," which had
prompted him to begin rewriting it.[4] Unfortunately, no scholar has
ever been able to peruse the manuscript. In 1878 or 1879, when the
plan of the novel had become clear in his mind, Verga prepared for
himself a detailed outline comprising a chronology of the action as
well as a delineation and definition of the main characters.[5] In accordance with the principles of *verismo*, he placed the entire series
of events within a very precise historical context, to the point of
hinging it on a set of dates. Such a time frame was obviously intended to give the feeling of actually relating "human documents."
The action was to begin in September 1865 and to end in February
1875—a decade of great political change and of immensely frustrated hopes.

It was the period immediately following the conquest of Sicily by
Garibaldi (1860) and of the subsequent annexation of the island to
the Kingdom of Italy, after centuries of feudalism under the
Spaniards and the Bourbons. As a result of the change, many had
expected radical social reforms, but they saw very little accomplished, and generally felt cheated in their expectations. The
novel does not go directly into these problems. Occasionally there is
a feeling of suspense between the old and the new: on one side the
nostalgia for the good old days, and on the other the emergence of
revolutionary hopes. But with the exception of the town clerk and
the pharmacist, the characters do not know much about politics.
Even when they are directly affected, rather than thinking of the
political system, they often take a fatalistic attitude, as if stricken by

an invisible and mysterious power. Such is especially the case of the old 'Ntoni Malavoglia. With the Kingdom of Italy, compulsory military service and new taxations had also arrived. Verga does indicate how deeply these obligations and impositions weigh upon even a traditional hardworking family of fishermen. In fact, one of the mainsprings of the novel is to be found precisely in the law of compulsory military service. But he presents the effects without debating the causes. He demonstrates that even though Master 'Ntoni does believe in earning his daily bread with the sweat of his brow, and does not advocate change, he still cannot remain immune to external forces.

When he listed his main characters, Verga also assigned to them a birth date, again for the purpose of establishing a precise scenario with a precise chronological progression. Master 'Ntoni, the patriarch, was born in 1801 and the youngest of his grandchildren in 1864. Although strongly rooted in tradition, the younger and necessarily the less stable members of the family were to be exposed to those yearnings for a better living that the historical moment was bound to awake in them. The definitions Verga gives to his characters ("honest," "hardworking," "vain," "lazy," etc.) generally correspond to the basic impression they leave in us; yet, after reading the novel, we feel in no position to categorize those people so simplistically as to encase them in an adjective.

The chronology adopted in the final version of the novel differs from the one in the original outline. Rather than in 1865 the action begins in 1864, and does not end in 1875, but in 1877. These deviations add smoothness to the sequence of events, which would otherwise have been squeezed into too short a period of time. The only date mentioned occurs at the beginning of the novel: December 1863, when young 'Ntoni "had been called for the service in the Navy" (p. 15). To this Verga adds that it is presently September. The other dates are only suggested. Toward the middle of the story, for instance, we find that it is 1866, because the family is informed that Luca had been killed in the battle of Lissa (fought between the Italians and the Austrians on July 20, 1866). Thus the time sequence, and the dates, are born of the lives of the characters as they unfold. But Verga's punctiliousness in prescribing all those details to himself is of interest insofar as it briefly shows him at work.

The title *I Malavoglia* was finalized when the novel was almost ready for the printer. In a letter accompanying the first half of the manuscript (August 9, 1880), Verga wrote to his publisher, Emilio Treves: "As to the title, it must be *I Malavoglia,* rather than *Padron 'Ntoni.*"[6]

The story of the Malavoglia family is also the story of the community in which they live. Hence the great number of minor characters and the apparent complexity of the plot. This factor has led many critics to assert that the real protagonist is the village, and not just a family—a view which I do not share. The Malavoglias live in the village and constantly interact with their friends and neighbors. It could not be otherwise. Thus, since they exert a definite influence on the Malavoglias' destiny, those villagers are, and have to be, an integral part of the story, and we must learn to know them. The village itself, Aci-Trezza, is on the eastern coast of Sicily, approximately ten miles north of Catania. Verga never describes it. Yet we feel as if we knew all its corners. From the very beginning we are immersed in its atmosphere, as if we had moved there and had become, rather than spectators, villagers ourselves.

The novel begins *in medias res,* without descriptions, without hesitations, and especially without waste of words. The first, truly unforgettable sentence provides the tone for the entire narration: "There was a time when the Malavoglias were as many as the stones of the old Trezza road." But now only Master 'Ntoni's Malavoglias are left in the village. After two pages, not only have we met them all, but we have grown familiar and friendly with them; we have even heard in the distance the echoes of the words with which the other villagers characterize and judge them. As there are no descriptions, there are no portraits. Everything is instantaneous— which is in sharp contrast with other nineteenth-century European novels, even the most famous ones. Verga gives us names and gestures, letting our imagination create the faces—and even the house itself. Whatever details we will learn, they will come exclusively from the speech and the gestures of the characters.

The novel is also the story of the house by the medlar tree—the very symbol of the family roots and of its unity—and of how it was lost. Together with the house there is the fishing boat, the *other* house, the home away from home, which makes survival possible. The grandfather, Master 'Ntoni, in full possession of the wisdom of the centuries, is the skipper. When he speaks, he utters proverbial maxims, because "the sayings of the ancients never lied" (p. 14). He is firmly planted in tradition. He knows that whatever is being done now has been done an infinite number of times in the past; that life consists in the perennial repetition of the same gestures for the same perennial purpose of surviving; that in our voyage we can travel only the path that has been found and marked from time immemorial; and whoever decides to change cannot reap anything but sorrow, and perhaps death. These fundamental truths can be expressed only with the words that have always contained them. He will say: "Without a helmsman a ship cannot sail," and: "Stick to your trade; you may not get rich, but you'll earn your daily bread." Speaking of the family he has some special definitions that clarify the function of the "helmsman": "Men are like the fingers of a hand; the thumb must act like a thumb, and the little finger must act like a little finger," or: "to pull an oar the five fingers must help one another" (pp. 13–14). Everyone has his place in life. Thus Master 'Ntoni's proverbs insist on the inevitability of social organization, with a man in charge who gives the orders. As is peculiar to primitive, natural wisdom, he derives his basic metaphor from the human body, from how it is structured, with each organ and each limb having a well-defined function, and being at the same time related to, or dependent upon, the functions of the others. Master 'Ntoni has always known this. In the family structure he is, of course, the "thumb." After him comes his son, Bastianazzo, who someday will himself be the "thumb"—but not yet, for "before being a Pope one must know how to be a sacristan" (p. 14). Then there is his son's wife, Maruzza, and finally the grandchildren in order of age: young 'Ntoni, who is about twenty; Luca, slightly younger; Mena, a grown girl who is very industrious and always busy around the house; and finally Lia, still too young for us to know how she will develop. They make their living fishing, and by cleaning, salting, and barrelling the catch before it is sold. They are a prosperous, if not rich, family, and are widely respected in town. They own their house and their boat, whose name is *Provvidenza*—which is supposed to be a good omen. It is mainly due to the respect commanded by this solid prosperity that the villagers call old 'Ntoni *Padron* (Master), which implies that he is a property owner.

II   *A Commentary on the Main Events*

After being drafted into the navy, young 'Ntoni Malavoglia is sent to Naples, where he is dazzled by the glitter of the ex-capital. Such a contact with a different and glamorous reality will slowly produce in

him the rejection of the hard life he has left behind. Meanwhile, in
the family they miss his strong arms. This, coupled with a generally
declining interest in fish by the people at large, causes the *Provvidenza* to remain idle. Therefore, the grandfather decides to take
advantage of a unique opportunity: there is a cargo ship at Riposto,
quite a few miles north of Aci-Trezza, buying up various types of
grains and beans. Padron 'Ntoni decides to purchase a load of
lupines on credit from the town usurer, Uncle Crocifisso, and then
have them ferried to Riposto and sold there at a profit. On a Saturday evening his son, Bastianazzo, with the helper Menico, sets out
with the *Provvidenza* and the cargo. In town there is a great deal of
talking about the Malavoglia's lupines. Verga uses this indulgence in
small talk to introduce a large number of villagers, letting their
personalities slowly emerge from their remarks. Before retiring,
Master 'Ntoni listens to the "bitter sea," while his granddaughter
Mena thinks at once of her father and of the cart-driver Alfio, whom
she secretly loves.

This scene ends chapter two, and constitutes one of the most
suggestive passages in the whole novel. Its images will recur again
and again throughout the text until their impact is both enhanced
and completed in the last pages. It is typical of the stylistic structure
of *I Malavoglia* that a set of images is presented and then restated in
particularly sensitive points in the narration, thereby becoming imbued with great depth and poetic power. Because of such quality it
is safe to assert that the structure of the novel is analogous to that of
a poem.

The day after is a bad September Sunday; the villagers watch the
fury of the sea and speak of the *Provvidenza;* Master 'Ntoni is silent
and restless. Just before evening falls we know that the boat has
gone under. Verga does not show us the storm that has swallowed
up Bastianazzo, Menico, and the cargo, simply because no one has
witnessed the disaster. But since everyone is a spectator, and a
participant, of the ruinous effects of such an event, he will give us
those effects. Verga believed that he could not be really true to life
unless he eliminated facts no one had been able to witness. It is
obvious that by adopting this method he managed to emphasize a
tragedy far more than by following in the footsteps of traditional
writers.

The lupine transaction puts the novel in motion. In it we must
recognize the hand of destiny, very much in the same way as in the

key incidents lying at the foundations of Greek tragedies. Master
'Ntoni maintained that no one should change his trade—"Stick to
your trade; you may not get rich, but you'll earn your daily
bread"—yet suddenly he is seduced by the glare of a commercial
venture, thereby turning from fisherman into businessman. This
implies a rejection of the basic principles that had guided his life, a
betrayal of the age-old wisdom he had inherited through "the sayings of the ancients" that "never lie." The only possible consequence
of Master 'Ntoni's deviation is the destruction of his family. Now the
cargo purchased on credit must be repaid. Meanwhile, Mena, the
older granddaughter, is left without a dowry and can no longer
marry, and the impending poverty causes the Malavoglias to lose
the respect of the villagers.

Everyone in the novel is governed by dire economic realities. The
ultimate symbol of such a tyranny is Uncle Crocifisso, to whom
Verga devotes chapter four—especially the first pages, in which the
personality of the usurer is delineated through a mixture of his own
and the villagers' remarks. He has money; he owns boats and fishing
gear. He is not a fisherman, but is ready to loan his implements to
those who need them, in the same way as he lends his money at a
weekly interest; he even buys up the fish wholesale, but it must be
weighed with his own scales. Everyone knows that he is a usurer,
that he exploits the villagers; yet everyone respects him—not only
because he is rich, but because he "sticks to his trade" (p. 54), and
does a good job of it. In a society where the struggle for survival is
the rule, he who manages to acquire money and property is not only
understood, but admired, by all those who would like to rise to the
same level and cannot.

Contrary to his norm, Uncle Crocifisso had given credit to the
Malavoglias without any guarantee. They owned property; besides,
he himself could not foresee such a disaster. But old Master 'Ntoni
"will have to pay," one way or the other (p. 55). Thus Uncle Crocifisso becomes for the Malavoglias an instrument of destiny, and
therefore he will cause further reversals to the family.

Against this grim background matures the tender love story of
Alfio Mosca, the cart-driver, and Mena Malavoglia, whom he sees
every evening from the landing in front of his door, when he returns
from the deliveries. During the day he imagines himself telling her
many things, but once he is before her he becomes tongue-tied.
Finally, one evening he manages to say: "Mena, I wish my donkey

were yours" (p. 73). The love between Alfio and Mena constitutes
one of the central themes of the novel; it is shy and inarticulate, but
deeply sensitive and moving—and destiny will never allow it to be
fulfilled.[7]

One day the old *Provvidenza* is fished out of the sea and is soon
being repaired. 'Ntoni returns from the draft, in spite of the fact that
by staying another six months he would have exempted his younger
brother, Luca. His return raises the hopes of the family, even
though Master 'Ntoni has to give Uncle Crocifisso all the family cash
to cover the interest on the debt. The Malavoglias are all working
hard now to earn enough to pay the caulker for patching up the
Provvidenza, and thus they cannot meet the Christmas deadline
with Uncle Crocifisso. The usurer's obsession with the debt keeps
growing, until he pretends to sell it to the village middleman,
Piedipapera, who sends the bailiff to the house by the medlar tree.
Although the house is hers, having invested her dowry in it,
Maruzza agrees that it actually belongs to the whole family. As a
result, the Malavoglias let Uncle Crocifisso and Piedipapera know
that they will pay their debt by all means, including giving up their
home, if necessary.

This is a momentous decision for the Malavoglia family, yet it is
reached quickly and simply, as if it were the only logical one. It is
the product of profound morality, of the impellent need to face up to
one's responsibilities and fulfill one's obligations. The Malavoglias
have a clear-cut way out: they could let their creditors wait—especially now that the *Provvidenza* is being repaired and soon can again
be brought out and filled with the bounty of the sea. But they
cannot; they know that the creditors are entitled to their money,
and must be paid or compensated in kind. The lawyer they have
consulted, and still more so the town clerk—who is the one to report
Master 'Ntoni's decision to Uncle Crofisso—will regard such a decision as insanely stupid. They have a different morality; they look
exclusively for personal gain; they make their living by taking, and
cannot understand those who are ready to give even when they do
not have to. The Malavoglias, on the other hand, live by their
conscience. The lupines they had bought from Uncle Crocifisso
were nearly rotten, and therefore worthless—yet this factor never
seems to be given any consideration by Master 'Ntoni. To him what
counts is the obligation he has incurred. The rest is not his business,
but Uncle Crocifisso's. The sad moral of this key episode is that

unswerving honesty often leads to great losses and even to total ruin, while the ruthless exploitation of others produces prosperity, and may even earn respect and esteem.

Christmas is not joyous for the Malavoglias, with the family further saddened by Luca's departure for the service. This was to be the last time they would see him, intimates the popular narrator, who anticipates part of the story by indicating that Luca would die young because he was good, wise, and frugal—a real Malavoglia—thereby establishing an implicit contrast with his brother 'Ntoni, about whom the reader now expects to hear much more.

It is unusual for Verga to let his unidentified and impersonal narrator anticipate future events. But it is normal, on the other hand, for him to smooth the transitions from one character to another by means of clues spontaneously rising from the dialogue. Chapter seven, for instance, will close with young 'Ntoni saying, "My brother Luca, there in the service, is better off!" (p. 122); and chapter eight will open with the narrator's comment: "Luca, poor fellow, was neither better off nor worse off; he was doing his best, as he had done at home, and expected nothing more" (p. 123). Other times the transition does not come from the dialogue, but from direct psychological associations. When a cart is heard rolling on the road, Alfio the cart-driver and his donkey immediately come to mind. It is Mena, as we know from chapter two, who regularly thinks about him each time she hears that noise. However, associating the carts with the cart-driver does not come naturally only to her but also to the villagers—although it is often no more than the superficial impression of external observers, as in chapter eight, where, by suggesting Alfio, the carts rolling in the night also suggest Mena, who is about to become engaged to Brasi Cipolla. It is a brief touch of gossip, but it serves to introduce the two Cipolla men, father and son, who pay a visit to the Malavoglias for the purpose of initiating the negotiations. Verga, by adopting this associational method of writing, can move with ease in the midst of an exceptionally large cast of characters. His original intension was, of course, to maintain his own impersonality—to be as objective as possible, and, therefore, to avoid completely the presence of the writer's hand. But the result is an extremely homogenous prose, very smooth and natural in all its sinews, removed from the literary models of the past and at the same time standing at the beginning of the modern narrative tradition.

The *Provvidenza* has been patched up; Master 'Ntoni dreams
about a return of prosperity, and Young 'Ntoni cannot understand
why he should work from morning to night while so many people in
the world can wallow in luxury. He complains about being a poor
devil and cannot accept his grandfather's philosophy that one's life is
determined by the conditions in which he was born. It is now, in
chapters eight and nine, that young 'Ntoni begins to assume great
significance, in the sense that he stands in direct opposition to his
grandfather. From here on, the two pivotal characters of the novel
will thus be the grandfather and the grandson, two antagonists who
represent two widely different generations, with a gigantic gap between them. With the lupine transaction, old Master 'Ntoni had
himself yielded to that "vague yearning for the unknown," to that
desire for being better off, of which Verga speaks in the introduction; but in the face of disaster he could pull himself together and
make recourse to the only remedy he knew: hard work. Young
'Ntoni, however, does not believe in attaining better living conditions slowly, with hard work, but being young, and therefore in a
hurry, he wants immediate improvement. "The vague yearning for
the unknown" will grow stronger and stronger in him until it will
coincide with this irresistible urge. He will reject all the principles
that have guided his family for generations, and will take risks he is
not prepared to face. Thus he will become one of the doomed who
fall by the wayside, but who are also an indispensable ingredient of
human progress.

Young 'Ntoni begins to court Barbara, the caulker's daughter, and
wants to marry her, but his grandfather rules that Mena must be
settled first. In fact, now that the *Provvidenza* is back at work,
Master 'Ntoni is planning to arrange for her marriage to Brasi
Cipolla. Alfio Mosca, as he becomes aware of such plans, decides to
move to another town, where (he says) he can make a better living.
But he also tells Mena that he cannot compete with Brasi Cipolla,
who is rich. The girl weeps in solitude. There is an engagement
ceremony, with great joviality among the villagers, while she cannot
bring herself up to full participation.

It is summer, and just then two sailors happen to stop at the
village tavern and to talk about a great naval battle that had taken
place in the Adriatic Sea, during which the famous battleship *Re
d'Italia* had been sunk. The villagers know that Luca Malavoglia had
been assigned to that ship, and rumors fly that he is dead. His

mother, Maruzza, cannot sleep at night for thinking of him; he becomes before her eyes the man in a story she had heard—who was dying of thirst in the middle of the sea, with so much water around. She herself seems to be continually thirsty. Finally she and Master 'Ntoni go to Catania to ascertain the facts. The impersonal clerk finds Luca's name on the list of the dead in action. Maruzza, struck again by destiny, can hardly withstand the blow; Master 'Ntoni becomes silent and distant, and the villagers see the new development as inevitable, for "when a ship is leaking, every wind blows against her" (p. 153). This is another tragic moment in the Malavoglia family, another link in the apparently interminable chain of their misfortunes. It is also a demonstration of how deeply the inhabitants of a remote village can be affected by the most distant events, even if they neither understand, nor care for, political and historical considerations. As a result of Luca's death, Uncle Crocifisso and his middleman, Piedipapera, claim the house by the medlar tree, and the Malavoglias are forced to move into a little rented cottage. Now that they have lost their house, the roots of their respectability, the villagers have only contempt for them: Master Cipolla even accuses Master 'Ntoni of having cheated him into agreeing to the marriage of his son with Mena, and promptly breaks the engagement; the caulker's daughter, Barbara, tells young 'Ntoni in no uncertain terms that all is finished between them. The Malavoglias themselves are aware of their new reputation and understand it; in fact, they even try not to show up in the village any longer.

The basic personal, as well as collective, human relations among the inhabitants of Aci-Trezza are predicated on money and property. Uncle Crocifisso and his likes will always be respected, if not always admired; they are solid and do not let themselves be fooled. But people such as the Malavoglias, who have allowed themselves to plummet from prosperity to near indigence, must be avoided like lepers. The fact that Master 'Ntoni had done all in his power to pay his debt, and that it had been his unflinching honesty to bring him to the present pass, is irrelevant. And so is the fact that Uncle Crocifisso had acquired the house by totally unscrupulous and dishonest means. He had won: he had demonstrated that he could take good care of his business; he was richer than ever, and as such he could always be of help in moments of need. If he had become rich at other people's expense, this was no ground for blame—it was rather a reason for admiring his skills, for there was no other known way of getting rich. Master 'Ntoni, on the other hand, had lost because of his bad judgment. He had let himself be trapped; as a result, he could no longer be trusted, and deserved no respect. And since the members of his family had no property with which to protect themselves in the future, no lasting relationship could be established with them by either Master Cipolla, or Barbara, or anyone else.

The old *Provvidenza* is all they have left, but the family works more stubbornly than ever, to make enough money to repurchase the house by the medlar tree. Young 'Ntoni, too, works with unexpected staunchness, as if guided by a rage, by a compulsion for revenge. He wants to show Barbara that he can make a comfortable living. But one day the Malavoglia men find themselves assaulted by a storm out at sea—the same kind of storm that had killed Bastianazzo, with the difference that then no one could report the details, for both the two people involved had died. Miraculously, the old boat does not break against the rocks. However, Master 'Ntoni is seriously injured, and for many days he lingers on the brink of death. He slowly recovers, the *Provvidenza* is again patched up, and the Malavoglia men return to sea. The catch is abundant and very much in demand, but Master 'Ntoni decides not to sell it until later in the year, when he will get a higher price.

Young 'Ntoni himself is elated with dreams of prosperity. Yet there is a thorn inside him. He has gotten into the habit of spending his evenings at the local tavern, where he meets two young men who have been away from home for a few years, and now are richly dressed and spend money like water; they do not try to keep busy by catching and salting sardines. "When we have sweated and slaved to build the nest," he says to his family, "we won't have the millet; . . . we'll always be where we started" (pp. 210–11). And the grandfather answers: "What? You want to stop working? What would you like to do? To be a lawyer?" (p. 211). In Verga's world a lawyer is an exploiter of other people's toil, one who sells glib, empty words. Thus wanting to be a lawyer means betraying one's obligation to work, violating the sacred law whereby man must earn his bread with the sweat of his brow. Even young 'Ntoni must reply to his grandfather: "No! I don't want to be a lawyer!" *(ibid.)*.

But after meeting those two at the tavern, he "could think of nothing but of the life without worries and without work other people led . . ." *(ibid.)*. External circumstances conspire with his

"vague yearning for the unknown" and slowly help turn his restless-
ness into a compulsive desire to be "better off" by any means. Soon
he will make up his mind. With all the family projects, with all their
needs and their entire future depending on fishing, he says that the
catch is bound to become scarce and, therefore, "we'll always be
poor. I don't want this kind of life anymore. I want a change, for
myself and for all of you. I want us to be rich" (p. 212). Master 'Ntoni
stares at his grandson while trying to swallow his words; then he
exclaims: "Rich! Rich! and what'll we do when we are rich?" *(ibid.)*.
The old man cannot conceive of a different life, devoid of responsibilities and free from toil. He retorts that his grandson should stay
where even the stones know him, should not be afraid of hard
work—for "the good pilot proves himself in a storm" (p. 213). Young
'Ntoni is moved, but the day after he is again possessed with rest-
lessness. Finally his mother talks him into staying home.

Verga's young 'Ntoni is fundamentally good, attached to his family
and understanding of their needs. What he cannot understand is the
passive acceptance of an unrewarding and, to a large extent, hope-
less life. He believes that it is possible to find fortune elsewhere in
the world, and thereby to improve not only his personal lot, but the
lot of his whole family. He fancies opportunities of material better-
ment, but he does so nebulously, without aiming at a specific target.
His inner motivating forces are essentially the same as those of many
enlightened poor, who rebel against the establishment because they
can no longer stand being confined in straitjackets, and finally end
up as social outcasts precisely because society does not tolerate
anyone who threatens to usurp material benefits rather than earning
whatever portion of them is within reach by following the rules.
Verga develops his character slowly and carefully, so that whatever
happens to him appears natural. Young 'Ntoni seems to carry his
destiny within himself; at times he may ignore it, even negate it, but
ultimately he will not be able to resist it. Circumstances will, of
course, favor the work of this destiny, just as in ancient tragedies,
but he will be the one to choose it by taking the fatal step. Yet the
reader cannot help being moved with both compassion and admiration for young 'Ntoni, a man who in his way, and with the serious
limitations imposed on him by his background, could envision a
mode of living that would be possible only many decades later—and
feel it in his bones. It was to be men like him—though much better
prepared and more practical in their objectives—that over a long
period of years would manage to make a reality out of his dreams.

Verga himself must have had the indistinct perception that with 'Ntoni he was creating a man projected towards the distant future. At the end of chapter ten the pharmacist speaks of his favorite subject (social revolution) and adds that "new men" are needed to carry it out. The town clerk rebukes him by drowning in sarcasm the names of some of these "new men," especially 'Ntoni Malavoglia, whom he judges irresponsible and inept (p. 206). Through the town clerk Verga voices his conservative conviction as to how one should stick to his trade without being seduced into unproductive fantasies. But this "new man" label suddenly, if sarcastically, attached to young 'Ntoni, may indeed signify Verga's unconscious historical perception of his character.

With the sudden outbreak of cholera and with the people who can afford to flee to the countryside, no one is buying sardines. The Malavoglias are left with their barrels full, and with a heap of collapsed dreams. As their savings are slowly being depleted, Maruzza helps the family by going about the countryside to deliver fresh eggs and bread. One evening she returns home with the disease in her system, and by morning she is dead. Again fate inexorably strikes the one who steps out of the assigned groove. Like Master 'Ntoni and Bastianazzo at the beginning of the novel, Maruzza too changes her trade to take up a business—and thus she too, as well as the entire family, is punished.

As a result of this tragedy, young 'Ntoni puts his departure plan into action and leaves the village to look for his fortune. Mena gets his things ready and thinks of her beloved Alfio, of where he could be with his cart. As when her father was out at sea with the lupines, her mind again lingers on the two most important men in her life as if they were one and the same person: then it was her father and Alfio; now it is her older brother and Alfio. Only many years after the novel was written, Freudian psychology would explore such subconscious associations—which may once more prove how a great writer's intuition can grasp instinctive but hidden human reactions long before they are recognized by the impersonal eye of the scientific researcher.

With young 'Ntoni gone and the family reduced to only the grandfather, the boy Alessi, the girls Mena and Lia, Master 'Ntoni realizes that he and his youngest grandson can no longer man the *Provvidenza,* and decides to sell it to Uncle Crocifisso, who also gets all the fishing gear for very little money. Thus the other Malavoglia house too, their home away from home, is gone. Master 'Ntoni feels this new loss in his own body, as if his vital organs were being savagely torn from him: "When they carried off the nets, the harpoons, the poles, and everything else, it was as if they were ripping his guts from his body" (p. 232). Those fishing implements were indeed like extensions of his own person.

Now Master 'Ntoni and Alessi take a job on Master Cipolla's boat. But while they sit home at night, the old man speaks again of the house by the medlar tree, of when they will buy it back, and of when the girls will be married and settled; that day he will be happy to close his eyes forever. He is indeed Verga's hero; when his entire world collapses around him, he stands like a giant, indomitable in his courage, unbending in his faith in life. He knows of no real despair, he is never depressed. To him misfortunes are the work of fate and, if fate strikes, man must pull himself to his feet and go on living.

Young 'Ntoni is different. He does not accept the same principles and becomes the victim of all the contradictions he carries within himself; thus he does not belong to either the past or the present. He has now been away for some time, and the whole village expects him to return rich. But suddenly he is back home, ragged and poor, and ashamed to show up in the streets. The family is happy to have him back; by working together, they can now earn more money. But 'Ntoni does not believe that a comfortable future can be built on the present foundations. His convictions about the injustice of the world have strengthened. He does some light work, but does not like having to take orders. Soon he begins to spend his time at the tavern, where he is befriended by the keeper, Santuzza, who because of him throws out her longtime lover, the sergeant of the *carabinieri*, Don Michele—who takes his revenge by courting Lia, 'Ntoni's younger sister.

The new development generates a great deal of gossip in the village. As in the second and fourth chapters, Verga's ear is keenly attuned to the villagers' small talk. Both through the dialogue and indirectly in the narrative stream, he relates the impressions and the comments of his numerous characters so that we receive the story from their lips. This gives us the illusion of being ourselves involved in the events of Aci-Trezza. But to the writer it represents a strategy for developing his characters smoothly and without resorting to definitions of his own. At this point, the man on whom Verga concentrates more than on anyone else is the pharmacist, who continues with his pronouncements: that the system does not work, and that people like Don Michele, who spends his time courting the girls, should be eliminated.

From here on the events progress rapidly. Santuzza soon tires of supporting young 'Ntoni and takes Don Michele back. 'Ntoni joins a group of smugglers who are looking for a pigeon. Don Michele tells the Malavoglia girls that their brother is going to be caught, for the chief of the gang, Piedipapera, will always land on his feet. But 'Ntoni does not listen. One night 'Ntoni and the sergeant have a fight before the tavern, which is continued another night when Don Michele and the other customs guards are determined to catch the smugglers. During the raid, the smugglers disappear, except 'Ntoni, who finds himself face to face with Don Michele, and in a fit of rage knifes him in the chest and is immediately arrested. As usual, the experienced members of the gang have utilized the inexperienced one for cover. Master 'Ntoni is thunderstruck as he discovers the new disaster that has befallen the Malavoglia family. But again he pulls himself together, goes to the lawyer, and gladly spends all the money he has slowly and doggedly saved to buy back the house by the medlar tree; for he knows that "the good pilot proves himself in a storm."

In town they say that fools get caught and that trouble comes only to those who look for it. But when many of them are subpoenaed to the superior court of Catania, they become worried and less talkative. To them being involved with the Law can bring nothing but bad tidings. Even the pharmacist, who holds a doctorate, maintains that to the Law we must always say that we do not know anything.

This attitude has deep historical roots. Sicily and Southern Italy in general had been under foreign domination for millennia. The people had been constantly abused and oppressed, with the consequence that the new generations had inherited an indelible distrust of the government and of all its representatives. Even Don Michele was often called a stranger, an exploiter, and a "pig," who filled his stomach by gobbling up the fruit of other people's work and whom no mother would allow her daughter to marry. Now that the Law is upon them, the villagers feel that it has not been enough to stay away from it and mind their own business. They have not been looking for trouble, yet they discover that they cannot help being affected by the trouble that has hit one of their kind.

Nearly the entire village attends the trial. Master 'Ntoni, lost in the crowd, listens to the defense lawyer say that there was no smuggling, since 'Ntoni and Don Michele had been simply fighting over a woman. And when that same lawyer goes on to state that 'Ntoni Malavoglia had intended to cleanse and restore the honor of his family—for Don Michele had seduced his sister Lia—the old man cannot hear anything any longer. Some of the people sitting nearby carry him out of the courtroom, thinking that he has had a stroke. They manage to revive him, and later they inform him that his grandson was sentenced to five years of hard labor.

The reference to an affair between his granddaughter Lia and Don Michele is the worst blow for Master 'Ntoni. The lawyer, with his peculiar logic, had intended to defend his client. But as is often the case, he had not realized that by so doing he was ruining his client's entire family. He had utilized a common Sicilian line of defense, without being interested in whether or not his statements were based on the truth, and without considering that in that same Sicilian society those statements, whether true or not, would be profoundly destructive. Thus he had unwittingly produced for the Malavoglias the last and most devastating of storms.

When told what has happened at the trial, Lia is stunned. Then, while her grandfather is being brought in on a cart, she walks out into the street and disappears from Aci-Trezza forever. In her Sicilian society, a girl is expected to guard her virginity until she is allowed to give it to a husband; any appearance of distraction or of looseness is blown out of proportion and equated with prostitution. Don Michele had been seen entering the Malavoglia house one evening as he went to tell the girls to urge their brother to steer clear of the smugglers. This had been enough for the villagers to think that Lia had behaved like a prostitute. Thus the girl's reputation had been permanently ruined, and she had no choice but to leave. In order to avoid the appearance of dishonor, she was actually forced to become a prostitute by the same people who abhor prostitution. It is one of the paradoxes of human interaction: in its blind intransigence, society often creates for the individual the very destiny that it vehemently condemns.

Master 'Ntoni is now a total wreck, the shadow of his old self. Uncle Crocifisso wants to sell him the house by the medlar tree, but he does not want it; he says that they do not need it, now that Mena cannot marry and the family no longer exists. Verga's towering hero has been finally vanquished. From the lupine affair to all the other disasters, he had never yielded to discouragement, but had always been ready to start all over again, his moral fiber stronger than ever. Not now. Poverty can be lived with and overcome, disgrace cannot. Now he can only invoke death as liberation.

Alessi takes a day job away from home to help support the family. Meanwhile, Alfio Mosca returns to the village with money and finds that things have changed so much that he almost regrets having returned. Finally Master 'Ntoni asks him to take him to the hospital on his cart, so that Mena and Alessi will not have to keep supporting him. One day, when the grandchildren go to carry him to the house by the medlar tree that they have repurchased, he is no longer there. The man who had spent all his life working for his family, and had constantly hoped to close his eyes in his own home, dies alone—and his body is quickly and coldly removed so that his hospital bed may be readied for someone else.

Alessi marries his childhood sweetheart. Through him the Malavoglia family appears to be about to be reestablished. In fact, we are left with the feeling that Alessi will become another Master 'Ntoni, equally solid in his moral commitments and beliefs. If anything, he will do better than his grandfather. It seems apparent that now this is for Verga the only possible road to progress: to erect a new building on old foundations. By projecting the rebirth of the family through Alessi, he reaffirms his faith in hard work and in traditional values. Survival, and even comfort, are achievable exclusively within the framework of specific rules, which coincide with the harmonious interdependence of the various segments of the social group. To break, or simply to alter, the delicate balance that ties people together is tantamount to extending an invitation to disaster.

One day Alfio Mosca asks Mena to marry him. The girl still loves him, but cannot say yes, because of the disgrace her sister has brought to the Malavoglia women. To this the cart-driver can only reply: "Cursed be the fate that has caused so many troubles!" (p. 323). As in the case of Lia, Mena's and Alfio's destiny is dictated by the severe laws on which the social structure of Aci-Trezza rests. Some of these laws may be viewed as oppressive prejudices; yet they constitute an integral part of what allows that very social structure to exist. We have found that in the village there is a precise caste system, based on money and property ownership, which cannot be in any way subverted without creating serious dislocations

and confusion: everyone belongs with his own kind, and marriages
are arranged among peers, so that well-to-do families can preserve,
and even expand, their wealth. On the other hand, sexual integrity
is expected of every girl who aspires to marriage, irrespective of her
economic condition. But as their financial status determines the
place of all the members of a given family on the social ladder, so the
disgrace of a woman affects the reputation of her close female relatives. Such a situation must be viewed as a remnant of the tribal
system, when the sins of one member were visited on the entire
tribe, and often also on future generations.

Alfio and Mena's moving and sad story is a good illustration of
these points. At first Alfio, who is poor, is in no position to marry
Mena, the daughter of the owners of a house and a boat, and has to
accept her being engaged to Brasi Cipolla, who is well-to-do. But
after a number of years Mena is poor and Alfio is well off; yet they
cannot marry either. Should they marry, the villagers would say that
Alfio's wife is a prostitute's sister, one who may have the same
inclinations in her blood—and the husband himself would be
ridiculed and despised. Thus Mena must withdraw to the attic of the
house by the medlar tree, "like an old pot that has been put away"
(p. 322), and devote herself to Alessi's children.

One evening after dark, young 'Ntoni returns home. He is tired
and hungry. Alessi and Mena feed him and offer him a bed. But he
asks about Lia, and as no one answers, he understands: "Don't you
see that I must go?" (p. 325). He knows that he must expiate alone.
And he adds: "Then I didn't know anything and didn't want to stay;
now that I know everything I must leave" (p. 327). It is the inarticulate but profound conclusion of five years of thinking—while in
jail—that to realize one's aspirations it is necessary to work hard and
to adhere to certain fundamental principles, for blind rebellion to
one's destiny activates another and much heavier destiny. He seems
to have learned the human need, and the significance, of construct-
ing one's life in harmonious interaction with others—and with an
environment. Thus he leaves the house, crosses the deserted village, and goes to sit on a retaining wall by a vineyard to wait for
dawn. It slowly comes. 'Ntoni hears the familiar sounds and sees the
old fishing boats. Everything as it used to be. Life continues with
the same voices and the same gestures, as if nothing ever happened.
It is time to go. He picks up his bundle and walks away, alone with
his alienation.

This is the end of the novel. We are left with the feeling that young 'Ntoni is embarking on a long and mysterious journey, as if he were leaving not Aci-Trezza, but the planet itself. He will wander in the vacuum he has created by pulling up his roots from the common humus and by negating the wisdom of generations. But he will remain with us, not only as the personification of that "vague yearning for the unknown" and of that desire for an "easier life" of which Verga speaks, but mainly as an intensely complex human being, destined to be destroyed by his own unbridled and untimely aspirations.

III   *A Note on Style*

The foregoing commentary is limited to the major events and themes. Of the forty-nine characters constituting the novel and the village, only those are mentioned that carry a pivotal significance in the action. The others, however, cannot be dismissed as unimportant, for they too are constantly present. They always behave in consonance with a destiny that is born of their background and environment. Verga never indulges in the expectation of his readers. In romantic novels, for instance, the hero who leaves his hometown to seek his fortune would normally return rich, and thus be finally able to realize his dreams. 'Ntoni Malavoglia, on the other hand, returns shoeless and in rags, poorer than when he left. This outcome is determined by that stringent logic of the human reality that Verga cannot deflect or modify, without renouncing his artistic ideals and without ignoring the inner substance and the destiny of his character.

The entire novel is constructed with a supreme sense of equilibrium. Every chapter is magnificent in itself, but it cannot be separated from the rest, very much like the five fingers of Master 'Ntoni's hand. The interaction between events and style is prodigiously effortless. Reading is like following the movements of life itself as it reaches the most distant capillary ramifications. Everything is obvious—that highly difficult "obvious," which only the greatest artists can attain. With *I Malavoglia* Verga came as close as conceivable to creating the perfect novel.

I have already indicated that Verga invented a language in which his poor and illiterate people could live and express themselves with fully personal implications, so that he could narrate in their words, thereby adopting a technique that later would lead to the interior monologue. In *I Malavoglia,* however, this technique is already considerably more complex than it was to be when fully developed by the twentieth-century novelists, in that it is not applied to individual characters only, but to an entire village. At this point I would like to present a few examples of Verga's style, even though I am conscious that on the one hand they are not sufficient to communicate the intricate expressive texture of the novel, and that on the other it is nearly impossible to convey its nuances through a translation.

First let us consider what may appear to be a descriptive passage. It occurs at the beginning of chapter three, when everyone knows that Bastianazzo is out at sea with the lupine cargo.

After midnight the wind had begun to make a hell of a racket, as if all the cats in town were screaming on the roof, and to shake up the shutters. You could hear the sea bellowing around the Farallon rocks, as if all the oxen of Sant'Alfio's Fair had gathered there, and the day came up blacker than the soul of Judas. In short, an ugly September Sunday—that treacherous September that suddenly hurls the sea at you, like a gunshot in the middle of the cactuses (p. 45).

The sudden fury of the wind and of the sea—which at the end of the previous chapter could be heard "snoring" quietly—is offered to us in the villagers' everyday experience. They had heard the screaming of the cats and the bellowing of the oxen at Sant'Alfio's Fair; these were familiar sounds, of suffering and despair, often fraught with bad omens. For them the blackest black possible was something they could only see through their imagination, the vicious color of the soul of Judas, which by spontaneous and "obvious" associations is followed, in their minds, by the idea of treachery. Verga's series of associations—one smoothly eliciting the other and often in consonance with the popular tendency to hyperbole—clearly spring from the invisible narrator's and the villagers' very lives. Even the syntax—which consists in the juxtaposition of the metaphors referring to commonly known facts—is theirs. But in these metaphors lies the thought of Bastianazzo at the mercy of a sea that supplies the means of survival, but that can also kill (as now may be the case).

At the beginning of chapter four the invisible popular narrator tells us of the predicament of the Malavoglia family by characterizing Uncle Crocifisso—in his own terms, in the terms of the villagers, and especially in those of Uncle Crocifisso himself.

The worst was that they'd bought the lupines on credit, and Uncle Cro-cifisso didn't want "fine words and rotten apples." That's why they called him Dumbbell, because when people tried to pay him with talk he was deaf in that ear, and used to say that "the creditor worries about the credit." He was a good old devil, and made his living by lending money to his friends. He had no other trade, and so he was all day long in the square, his hand in his pockets, or leaning against the church wall, always wearing the same dilapidated jacket, and you wouldn't have thought he was worth a penny; instead he had as much money as you wanted, and if somebody asked him for twelve *tari*, he lent them right away, but with collateral, for "if you lend money without collateral, you lose your friend, your money, and your wits," and with the understanding that he would have them back by Sunday, in solid silver and with a *carlino* of interest, as was only right, for "in business there is no friendship." He also bought all the catch, at a discount, when the poor fisherman needed cash at once; but then the fish had to be weighed with his own scales, which were as false as Judas—said those who find fault with everything and have one arm long and the other short, like Saint Francis. . . . In fact, he was Providence itself, if you were in bad straits . . . (p. 45).

This is the most extensive, the most intricate, and the most dynamic commentary on any character to be found in the novel. We can actually observe Uncle Crocifisso busying himself in the village, and can hear him repeat his words over and over again. The expressions between quotations ("fine words and rotten apples" . . . "In busi-ness there is no friendship") are popular proverbial sayings, and as such they imply irrefutable truths. By making constant recourse to those sayings, Uncle Crocifisso astutely finds a common ground with his interlocutors and disarms them in advance, should they try to object to some of his stipulations. If the villagers accuse him of cheating with his scales, which are "as false as Judas," he can readily retort that those are the kind of people that find "fault with every-thing," who have "one arm short and one long"—the former to give and the latter to take—like the familiar statue of Saint Francis. Like his proverbs, Uncle Crocifisso's analogies are drawn from the village repertoire, and therefore are quick and to the point. He goes further: each time he manages to extract some money from his fellow men, he can define himself as "Providence" in person. And indeed he does have a beneficial function in Aci-Trezza, as is recog-nized even by those who have to give him their money: "with a *carlino* of interest, as was only right." The villagers say that "he was deaf in that ear," thereby repeating what they had heard him state

time and time again, and call him "Dumbbell"; they also inform us
that he dresses so poorly that "you wouldn't have thought he was
worth a penny." The invisible narrator pieces everything together
into a unit by contributing his own connective tissues, by putting all
the verbs in the past tense—typically the procedure from direct to
indirect speech—and by adding a touch of genial irony, whenever
there is a chance.

Verga does not always create so complex a prose, with so many
voices heard in its texture at once. More often he reflects the speech
of only one or two characters. Still in chapter four, we are in the
village church during Bastianazzo's funeral:

This time the Malavoglias were there, seated on their heels before the
coffin, and washing the pavement with their tears, as if the dead man were
really between those four boards, with his lupines around his neck—for
Uncle Crocifisso had given them to Master 'Ntoni on credit, because he had
always known him as an honest man; but if they now planned to swindle him
out of his property, with the pretext that Bastianazzo had drowned, they
were swindling Christ, as true as God! That credit was as sacred as the
consecrated Host, and he would lay those five hundred lire at the feet of the
crucified Jesus; but damn it! Master 'Ntoni would go to jail! There was the
law at Trezza too! (p. 54-55)

Traditionally, most of the above passage would have been written in
the form of a straight monologue. In fact, beginning with the words
immediately following his name, should we change all the verb
tenses to the present and all the verbal persons referring to him
from third to first, we would have Uncle Crocifisso's speech, with
his typical intonation and his peculiar exclamations of despair. In the
opening lines he is not as yet speaking; however, even there we
cannot escape the turbulent repercussions of his all-pervasive obsession with the debt. He is not able to understand the Malavoglias'
grief; he sees them cry, but to him their tears are shed for the wrong
reason. To him the real tragedy is not Bastianazzo's death, but the
loss of the lupine cargo, and consequently the probable loss of his
own money—about which the Malavoglias do not seem to be worried at all. It is at this point that Verga pronounces his name, as if to
tell us that he had been reporting about him all along. As a result,
suddenly Uncle Crocifisso seems to tower in the middle of the
church, speaking loudly and clearly, declaiming to the powers of
heaven and earth. He had granted credit to Master 'Ntoni, because

Master 'Ntoni had always been an honest man; but now . . . Uncle
Crocifisso unavoidably judges others according to his own immediate personal interest. Beneath his words there is also the fear of
having fallen into a trap. Thus the possibility of losing those five
hundred lire swiftly grows in his mind into a definite and inescapable fact. Soon it even leads him to contemplate foregoing that sum
of money altogether, should God himself so decree; but as he knows
that God can only decree in his favor, he goes on shouting inside
himself that Master 'Ntoni must "go to jail." It does not occur to him
that Master 'Ntoni is still an honest man and will do everything in
his power to repay the debt. Autosuggestion has caused fear to
become a doubt and doubt to become a certainty, thereby blinding
its victim into greater and greater anger. In no other way than with a
brief interior monologue could the essence of this character have
been so fully disclosed. In his future works Verga will recreate
Uncle Crocifisso and will give him a new breadth by transforming
him first into Mazzarò and then into Mastro-don Gesualdo—the
most complex, the most ambitious, and to a great extent the most
unfortunate of all his "doomed."

Another quotation will suffice. This time it is young 'Ntoni, who,
after returning from his venture, must resign himself to earning his
daily wages by working for others.

Then there was that business of hiring out that he didn't like at all, he who
had been born a master, as his grandfather himself had said. To be ordered
around by those who had come up from nothing—and everyone in town
knew how they had made their money, penny atop penny, toiling and
sweating it out! He hired out only because his grandfather insisted, and
didn't have the heart to refuse. But when the overseer kept after him like a
dog, and yelled at him from the stern: "Hey, you there! What are you here
for?" he felt like hitting that overseer on the head with his oar, and he'd
rather spend his time repairing the fishing baskets and mending the nets,
sitting on the beach, his legs stretched out and his back leaning against the
rocks; for then, if he rested for a moment with his arms crossed, nobody
would say anything (p. 243).

Again the passage reproduces the words of the character. The syntax, in its aliterary and somewhat primitive simplicity, reflects
'Ntoni's mental wanderings to and from what is for him a foregone
conclusion. It is more straightforward than in the Uncle Crocifisso
passages, in which the prose structure—although on the surface

equally unsophisticated—recreates the devious reasoning of a man
who constantly needs to remind himself, others, and even God, that
to safeguard his own interest is no more than fulfilling a moral
commitment, and consequently it meanders from phrase to phrase
without being able to develop along logical lines.

Thomas G. Bergin observes that Verga's style "is artfully simple
and has a vividness that is unsurpassed in modern prose."[8] No other
definition could be more synthetically comprehensive or more accurate. Verga's efforts to eliminate all possible interventions by having
the story emerge from the dialogue and by letting the characters
themselves enucleate their own inner motivations throughout an
entire novel, led him to the creation of a narrative which stands at
the origin of a tradition.[9]

But it was precisely because of its totally new style and language
that I Malavoglia failed to attract the readers and the critics. The
few reviewers were clearly disconcerted. To them Verga was still
the author of the romantic and passionate stories of his youth. They
found the book monotonous and the language unacceptable. One of
them went so far as to state that it should have been written in
Sicilian.[10] It was a classic example of how great works of art—being
projected toward the future—cannot be appreciated by contemporary readers, who are attuned to those rhythms and to those expressive forms that are as easily perceivable as they are habitual.

The only article in praise of I Malavoglia was authored by Verga's
friend Luigi Capuana, who maintained that the novel was indeed a
work of great significance, and exalted its "naked" objectivity. He
identified the reason for the public's apathy in the fact that the
readers were accustomed to saccharine stories dressed in Romantic
rhetoric, and correctly predicted the novel's future triumphs.[11]
However, the greatest critic of the time, Francesco De Sanctis,
disregarded Verga altogether. In 1879 he had declared that writers,
rather than "talking" themselves, should "make things talk."[12] But
then he failed to recognize the masterpiece which far surpassed his
anticipations. Another noted critic, Francesco Torraca, reviewed I
Malavoglia by essentially limiting himself to underlining its social
implications and thereby putting it side by side with the already
celebrated inquest on the conditions of the Sicilian peasants by L.
Franchetti and S. Sonnino;[13] to his credit, he insisted that the writer
was not an economist but an artist.[14] The other critics either expressed negative opinions or said nothing.

Verga could not quite understand such a cold official response. "*I Malavoglia* is a fiasco, a great big fiasco," he wrote to Capuana on April 11, 1881. "The worst is that I am not at all convinced that it is a fiasco; if I were to write that book all over again, I would write it exactly as it is."[15] To Carlo Del Balzo, who had severely censured the style and the language, Verga reiterated: "Were I to write *I Malavoglia* all over again, I would write it exactly in the same way; its form [i.e., its style and its language] seems to me completely necessary and inherent to the subject matter."[16] A few months later, when his French translator, Edouard Rod, asked permission for a version of the novel, but with some cuts and omissions, Verga answered: "I would only beg you to leave the text intact. . . . I feel that in *I Malavoglia* I have written neither a line nor a word that could be considered superfluous."[17] It appears unquestionable that Verga was perfectly aware of what he had accomplished, that he knew that his characters and their human vicissitudes could exist only within the language and the stylistic structures he had selected.

The first comprehensive article on Verga in general and on *I Malavoglia* in particular was published by Benedetto Croce in 1903. But it did not constitute the full recognition one might have expected at that late date. Croce complained that the language was faulty in all of Verga's works and then he defined the novel as a broader canvas than the short stories, and added that "perhaps" it was to be preferred to *Mastro-don Gesualdo*. He did, however, suggest that from *I Malavoglia* one receives the impression of a powerfully unitary work.[18] Croce's article, although rather circumspect, was of great importance insofar as it became the precursor of Luigi Russo's criticism, whose 1919 volume[19]—totally recast in 1933 and substantially enlarged in 1941—solidly demonstrated the greatness of Verga's mature fiction, and placed *I Malavoglia* on the same level as the few European masterpieces of the last century. The novel had thus finally gained some of the recognition it deserved, even though many more years had to pass before official criticism could perceive the originality of its expressive structures.[20] In our days Marxist critics, by mainly viewing *I Malavoglia* as a social document, have unknowingly reverted to Francesco Torraca's statements. Romano Luperini,[21] for example, takes issue with Verga for avoiding any direct condemnation of, and therefore for apparently accepting, the social institutions of his time.

CHAPTER 4

A Drifting Interlude

I   Il marito di Elena (Helen's Husband)

IN spite of Luigi Capuana's reassurances that *I Malavoglia* was by no means a fiasco—but rather that it was the readers and the critics who were failing and sooner or later would have to change their minds[1]—Verga could not accept that the book did not sell. He thus decided to complete a new novel and quickly publish it, for the purpose (as he put it) of paying the rent.[2] With *Il marito di Elena* he forced himself to postpone *Mastro-don Gesualdo*, the continuation of the *I Vinti* (The Doomed) series, and to attempt to meet the questionable taste of a potentially large segment of the reading public. We do not know whether in Verga's personal history this novel had been initiated, and then abandoned, during the period of *Eros*, or if it was conceived and written in full during a few months in 1881. In both plot and style, it does indeed remind us of the better of his early bourgeois works—such as especially *Eros*, which it resembles in the deliberate analysis of the characters' so-called psychology. But having been written six or seven years after *Eros*, and following the great achievement of *I Malavoglia*, the new novel has generally constituted a grave problem for the critics, who have often dismissed it as either an anomaly or an accident.

Cesare Dorello, a poor but promising law student, falls in love with Elena, a young woman of the Neapolitan bourgeoisie, whose life revolves around dreams of love and luxuries. After Cesare's graduation, the two lovers elope and marry. Cesare is forced to work very hard, while Elena squanders all the money he earns. Slowly she becomes the victim of her own fantasies and yields to her romantic fascination for pseudo-poets and playboys. Blinded by love, Cesare cannot believe in the possibility of her having affairs, until he is forced to face the facts. One night he enters Elena's room in order to forgive her and beg her to remain with him. But she is startled and reacts with contemptuous fright. Feeling rejected, Cesare cries: "Ah, you don't love me anymore. . . . You are only afraid!", and kills her (p. 357).[3]

When Verga wrote *Il marito di Elena*, it was commonly believed that the novelist should direct his attention to the psychological reactions of his characters, thereby devoting his energies to the composition of "analytical" works. Verga himself, a few months after completing this novel, defined Edouard Rod's *Côte à Côte* as a "very effective analysis from which the personal drama rises spontaneously and almost of necessity," and then added: "Your novel proves to me more and more that the deepest impressions—those that must set us to thinking—come from the modest everyday dramas, among which we live without noticing."[4] In both these statements Verga seems to be giving the intentions that had stood behind his writing of *Il marito di Elena*. In the preface to "L'amante di Gramigna" he had insisted that the novel should develop with the same natural spontaneity as human passions—a principle that, if applied to psychological analysis, would produce a work mirroring the most elusive ripplings of the psyche without the intrusion of the author's hand. In *Il marito di Elena*, however, Verga does not succeed in bringing this ideal of impersonality to fruition. In fact, he is often present with expressions of either approval or disapproval, which ring as his own even when stylistically they may appear to be spoken by the invisible observer. Here is an example: "As a boy he had always been in the midst of that dignified poverty that paints all your actions in gray, and regulates them with those precise calculations that give great importance to riches, because of the painful and continuous contrast that there is between being [rich] and pretending to be" (p. 228). And, almost immediately after: "He knew that you have to dig and dig into your head, as if with a hoe, to be able to get to that degree," where Verga, although resorting to a rather popular language, gives the impression of referring to one of his personal experiences—when he himself was a law student at the University of Catania and decided to drop out.

Still more unfortunate are other intrusions which unavoidably disturb any smooth reading of the novel, such as: "Thus the flood of life picked them up again and carried them farther and farther from each other" (p. 245); "Only God knows what went through the minds of that husband and wife, who were sitting so close to each other on the same balcony" (p. 296); and: "Who can analyze the ultimate consequences of the simplest remarks?" (p. 265). This last quotation indicates that the author has intellectualized his characters without really being able to make them live naturally and effortlessly. Such an exclamatory-interrogatory sentence is vague and without object. Imprecision is one of the weaknesses of the novel. It is rooted in the author's inability to view his characters and their vicissitudes from a certain distance, with the result that the characters themselves are described rather than presented. Verga intends to analyze their psychology, and yet he is unable to go beyond a somewhat reflective, at times vacuously emphatic and exclamatory, commentary from the outside. In the last pages of the novel, he proceeds through a string of exclamations on the assumption that they reflect Cesare's psychological condition in that tragic moment. Instead they sound almost like the transcription of the reactions of a superficial observer, of one who is not present but is told about the event in a moment of inebriated elation. Thus what could have been an intense drama is translated into light melodrama—and a rather poor one at that.

In some ways we can state that *Il marito di Elena* re-elaborates the story of Ieli and Mara by transposing it onto a different [higher?] social level—even if it is not the lover to be killed but the wife. Cesare is as passionately and as blindly in love with Elena as Ieli is with Mara. At the end Cesare kills Elena in a sudden flash of realization—as an equally sudden and substantially similar feeling of discovery compels Ieli to kill Don Alfonso. Like the short story, the entire novel leads to that supreme moment in which the protagonist becomes aware of his rejection by the person to whom he has given all his life; therefore, he cannot help reacting violently as if to re-establish some sort of equilibrium. Yet the story is far better than the novel.

It seems rather strange that Verga should conceive of a work as being a psychological analysis only if it dealt with bourgeois characters. The psychologies of Ieli and Mara, of Mena Malavoglia and Alfio Mosca, as well as of the two 'Ntoni's and of Uncle Crocifisso, stand out with great evidence. A few words at the right time are enough to tell us everything about the emotional reactions of the characters. However, if Verga, as well as many other writers of his time, thought that psychological works should involve the bourgeoisie, it was probably because only the bourgeoisie read their novels and could identify with their characters. But misconception it was, and as such it kept forcing a writer to look for characters who often were not, so to speak, on the same wavelength as his own natural predilections.

Yet in *Il marito di Elena* there are some passages of great efficacy. Chapter four has two of them: the episode concerned with Cesare's relatives receiving the news of his elopement with Elena, and the pages devoted to his mother's journeying to Naples for the purpose of dissuading him from going ahead with his plans. The prime mover of both passages is the sense of despair produced by poverty. At one point his mother tells Cesare: "That's how it is! Were we rich, neither you nor I would now have this thorn in our hearts!" (p. 244). It is the most suggestive and the most typically Verghian of all the utterances in the novel. We are once more reminded of Enrico Lanti's remark to Eva that poverty has turned love into a luxury he can no longer afford; and at the same time we are offered the preview of one of the pivotal principles on which the fabric of "Pane nero" (Black Bread) rests: "The trouble is we're too poor to love each other all the time."[5]

The fundamental lack of detachment that to a great extent is responsible for the novel's weaknesses is rooted in Verga's attitude toward marriage and toward bourgeois women in general. Even though he did not disdain pursuing love affairs, Verga was basically a misogynist as far as bourgeois women were concerned. He respected the women of the working classes, for they contributed to the welfare of their families—while he viewed bourgeois females as parasites of their husbands, spending the money their husbands managed to put together with so much toil, striving to live in luxury, loafing from morning to night, nursing their sensuality and ready to betray the very husbands who were providing them with the means for such a comfortable living. Because of this attitude Verga unflinchingly avoided marriage all his life.[6] Elena is the personification of his concept of the bourgeois woman. Verga does not spare her his contempt. She behaves "like a great lady and is courted like a queen" (p. 280); at the beginning of one of her affairs she is "irritated for not being allowed that innocent game" (p. 286); "if her pride" is not satisfied, she is "in a bad mood all evening" (p. 289); and she is constantly full of "bourgeois vanity" (p. 342). Similar derogatory expressions occur throughout the novel.

As to Cesare, on the other hand, Verga harbors no contempt, but rather the compassion one feels for the innocent victim of blind selfishness—for a man who is full of love and devotion for the wrong object, who is good in his intentions but is also so naïve as to let himself be constantly deceived and exploited. In one instance, however, Verga seems to be losing his patience: "Yes, he still loved her, the damned fool!" (p. 346), and then he tries to characterize the nature of Cesare's reactions to his wife's love affairs: "He could feel jealousy in the manner the weak do—unable to break his chain, with such a vague hope that he couldn't even confess to himself that he could reconquer her love through constant generosity, devotion, and even indulgence" (p. 346). These comments are indisputably Verga's, even if Verga might intend them as belonging to his invisible popular narrator. In fact, while he attempts to identify the reasons for an attitude he cannot accept, he passes judgment on his character and implicitly rejects him. Thus his intolerance for marriage, his aversion for the women who become wives, and his dislike for the men who agree to become husbands, made it impossible for Verga to write with the necessary degree of objectivity. When the composition of the novel was already in an advanced stage, he must have perceived the extraordinary difficulty inherent in portraying characters he did not quite comprehend. In a letter to Capuana dated July 30, 1881, he asked: "As to *Il marito di Elena* . . . don't you think that certain topics carry bad luck with them?"[7]

It has often been stated that *Il marito di Elena* was inspired by Gustave Flaubert's *Madame Bovary,* especially because of the behavior of the respective women protagonists. It is, however, reasonable to assert that there is indeed very little similarity between the two novels. As Thomas G. Bergin writes, "*Madame Bovary* is, if you will, the tragedy of a bored woman; Verga's novel is the tragedy of a man married to such a woman."[8] Similarly, Luigi Russo sees *Il marito di Elena* as the drama of a man whose dreams of happiness "are destroyed by the vanity and the frivolity of his wife."[9] We may even recall that, upon reading *Madame Bovary,* Verga flatly told Capuana that he did not like it, even though it revealed the hand of a master. Then he added that in it there was only the realism "of the senses, with the passions of the characters lasting no longer than a sensation. . . . Additionally, the book is written by a skeptic . . . or by a man who has no established principles, which is worse."[10] He probably meant that in *Madame Bovary* the writer did not quite

understand his characters—a remark that ironically applies to the
Verga of *Il marito di Elena* rather than to the Flaubert of *Madame
Bovary* [11]

II *"Il come, il quando ed il perché"*
(The How, the When and the Wherefore)

In 1881 Verga appended to the second edition of *Vita dei campi*
this novelette, whose subject matter and development had no relationship with the stories collected in the volume of "Life in the
Fields"; it was, instead, born of the same spirit as that which had
produced *Eros* and *Il marito di Elena.* Yet, although it is stylistically
somewhat overemphatic and not free of banality, "Il come, il
quando ed il perché" is generally better than the novels—the narration remaining on a plain of smooth uniformity, with very few groping excursions on different expressive levels. Again Verga does not
hesitate to manifest his contempt for the female protagonist, especially in the opening pages. The story, in fact, begins with the
statement that Polidori and Maria Rinaldi loved each other—or
"thought" they loved each other, "which is often exactly the same
thing. . . . They were made for each other: Polidori enjoyed an
income of forty thousand lire and the reputation of being a dangerous playboy; Madame Rinaldi was a pretty and frivolous woman, and
had a husband who worked as much as ten people so that she could
live as if she did enjoy an income of forty thousand lire" (p. 227).
Polidori and Maria are about to initiate a torrid love affair when she
runs away, leaving Villa d'Este and returning to Milan, where she
learns that her husband had to rush to Rome because of a financial
reversal. She travels to Rome and arrives just in time to save her
husband from suicide. At the end of the story Maria's standard of
living is much more modest, and she is much wiser.

In the story there are many felicitous passages. Verga is particularly successful in registering step by step his protagonist's emotional involvement. The shortcomings, on the other hand, derive
from his occasional indulgence in viewing external factors from a
purely descriptive angle. A case in point is the spring morning of
the first appointment between the two lovers in the park, which
is felt as overflowing with such a pervasive sensuality as to invite
an uncomfortable comparison with a memorable noon hour in

"Nedda." In its entirety, however, the work may be seen as the result of the somewhat concentrated efforts of a fully matured talent.

III   Novelle rusticane *(Rustic Tales)*

This new collection of short stories was published in Turin in 1883. This time it was a great writer at his best—continuing on the path of *Vita dei campi* (which, at least in the title, the new volume strongly resembles) and of *I Malavoglia*. The majority of the stories were published during the second half of 1881 and the first half of 1882, and, significantly, they were written during the very months Verga worked on *Il marito de Elena*. Again he deals with the trials and tribulations, the dreams and the disappointments, the few joys and the many sorrows of his Sicilian peasants, whose main struggle is, as for the Malavoglia family, to secure both physical and emotional survival. Contrary, however, to the Malavoglia family's situation, this survival is sought *per se*, irrespective of justice, honor, and self-respect. Unlike the heroes of *Vita dei campi* and unlike young 'Ntoni Malavoglia, who are able to rise in rebellion against the tyranny of destiny or the iniquity of a neighbor who usurps their rights and their property, the protagonists of *Novelle rusticane* no longer yield to the desire to dominate or destroy their oppressors, but accept being victimized by both nature and society, as though by fate itself. They are indeed "Doomed." As a result, tragedy never explodes. Even when, as in "La libertà," the peasants take the law into their own hands and eliminate their oppressors, they become fearful and speechless as soon as they realize that they have also tried to eliminate centuries of social structures—those structures without which they themselves could not survive. Thus what has begun as an uprising of heroes ends with the unnerved protagonists herded together like common criminals. Generally the characters of *Novelle rusticane* are victims of a slow deterioration and are finally undone by the very elements that allow them to exist.

There is also a great deal of humor in these *Novelle*, but it is a dark and bitter humor—the result of a pessimistic outlook on life by a writer who has grown both fatalistic and unable to find any redeeming traits in his own people's actions. He seems to insist that the hand of fate weighs heavily on each of us, and there is nothing we can do to lift it. Yet the main theme of the book is economic: property and money on one side, and poverty and near starvation on the other; those who have and those who have not, with the latter being subjected to the former, and with all of them pursued by a relentless destiny. The style, enriched with all the discoveries of the previous "Sicilian" books, is supple and complex, and the people's lives are perfectly fused with the heavy atmosphere of the desolate countryside; they are created and accompanied by the rhythm of the words, and by the slow, intriguing music of sentences that are often imbued with such continuity as to reach symphonic proportions.

"Malaria," first published in August 1881, introduces some of the main themes of the volume and evokes the climate in which all the people live. It is a large musical canvas with the characters sketched against a desolate background.

You'd think you could touch it with your hands—as if it came from the rich smoky earth, there, everywhere, all around the mountains that close it in, from Agnone to the snow-capped Etna—stagnating in the plain like the heavy suffocating heat of July. . . . When the herd's bell resounds in the great silence, the wagtails fly away silently, and the herdsman himself, he too yellow with fever and white with dust, opens his swollen lids for an instant, lifting his head in the shade of dry rushes.

Malaria gets into your bones with the bread you eat, and when you open your mouth to speak, as you walk on the roads that stifle you with dust and sun, and you feel your knees give way, and you sink down on the saddle as your mule ambles along, its head drooping. . . . Malaria snatches up the villagers in the deserted streets and nails them in front of the doors of their houses plasterless from the sun; and they shake with fever under their overcoats and under all the bed blankets piled up on their shoulders (p. 291).

It is a great beginning—filled with the all-pervading essence of the disease, which is indeed made of the same substance as the air (*malaria* is the Italian for "evil air"). It is everywhere. No one can see it, and yet everyone is aware of its presence. Or it may appear to be like a blindly cruel mythical monster, before which all living creatures unite in an effort to defend themselves. The passage, in its paratactic, juxtapositional structure and in its melancholy rhythm, does indeed reflect this effort to survive and at the same time tells us that it is all in vain.

Now we are prepared to meet some of the victims:

When the sweat of the fever leaves someone stiff on the corn-husk mattress, and there is no need for quinine or eucalyptus tea any more, they load him on the hay-cart, or on the donkey's packsaddle, or on a ladder, any way they can, with a sack over his face, and they go to lay him by the lonely little church, under the spiny cactuses, whose fruit for that reason no one eats. The women cry together in a group, and the men look on, smoking (p. 293).

Malaria has won, and the surviving men can muster a feeling of self-defense only in the immobility of their fatalistic, stony silence. This is how, Verga adds, they had carried off *massaro* Croce, who before dying had reassured those around him that his children would be financially well cared for.

In the general architecture of the story—which consists of a series of episodes tied together by that invisible and cruelest of monsters called malaria—*massaro* Croce's brief, disheartening appearance represents the connective link between the diffuse atmosphere of the first pages and the human figures of the rest; it also serves to introduce those figures, who have essentially become integral parts of a landscape that permits them to survive ("where there is malaria the land is blessed by God. In June the wheat ears fall to the ground from the weight, and the furrows smoke as if they had blood in their veins, as soon as the plowshare goes into them in November," p. 293)—but that also drags them into death.

Thus Carmine, the tavern keeper by the lake, had lost all his five children to malaria, and had seen all his wives die, one by one, although he had kept getting married, because without a wife a tavern cannot go. And since they had built the railroad, he had also lost all his customers, so that, after fifty-seven years, he could no longer pay the rent, and had been evicted. To survive he had to accept a job as a flagman with that hated railroad which had destroyed his business. Carmine now envied all those people who were filing by in the comfort of a train; they were "like pieces of the city rolling by in front of you, with all the lights of the streets and the sparkling stores" (p. 298). Then he understood the difference between their destiny and his own: "Ah! for those people there just isn't malaria!" (p. 298).

There was also a man malaria had not wanted, because "it didn't know what to do with him" (p. 295). It was Cirino, the Idiot, who slept in ditches and lived on charity. He was as yellow as saffron and kept singing at the top of his lungs under the sun that hammered down on his bare head, and ran shouting after the train, his arms gesticulating in the air. That, and nothing else, was life for him.

Malaria had ruthlessly pushed him down to the lowest level of abjection, and had left him there—very much in the same way as it had destroyed Carmine's family and then had forced him to make a living by brandishing an idiotic flag.

"Malaria" is a tale of solitude and of misery without any possibility of rebellion. Death is constantly present and strikes down only the poor—the rich being always well sheltered and protected. Reading the story is almost like visiting the antichambers of the palace of death, with its crowd of human beings awaiting their turn to disappear.

In the same Plain of Catania Verga sets another of his most famous short stories. However, "La roba" (Property) is not intended as a vast fresco of an entire region and its people, but as the robust portrait of a man. Mazzarò, guided by an unfaltering willpower and by great cunning, has become the owner of all the lands and herds and groves in sight. This time Verga's theme is the compulsive drive for riches—how it totally possesses a man, how it produces only isolation, and how it ultimately offers no more than emptiness and despair—with his protagonist looking both heroic and absurd.

"La roba" opens with a grandiose prelude, anchored exclusively to a single recurrent note, "Mazzarò's." At first the general cadence of the prose appears similar to that of the beginning of "Malaria," but it is precisely the insertion of that recurrent note that gives it a completely new dimension. Not only does it immediately assure us that the story is centered on a single character, but it also staunchly asserts that the character has been translated into the world around him, his own property. "With the reechoing of Mazzarò's name, the theme of the countryside is punctuated by a specific rhythm, as it begins to be born and to develop, and to become 'Property.' "[12] Mazzarò owns everything that can touch our senses. And everything *is* Mazzarò:

It seemed as if even the setting sun, and the buzzing cicadas, and the birds flying short flights to go and nestle behind the clods, and the hoot of the horned owl in the woods, were Mazzarò's (p. 308).

That obsessive note soon becomes so overpowering that the reader suddenly feels that this man is as big and as vast as the earth itself: "It seemed as if Mazzarò were stretched out as big as the earth and you walked on his belly" (p. 308). At this point, after seeing Mazzarò grow to such enormous proportions, the reader can hardly avoid asking: "But what kind of person is he?" Anticipating this hypothetical question, Verga—or rather the invisible popular narrator—offers the answer.

Instead, he was a puny little man, said the litter driver, and if you saw him you wouldn't have thought he was worth a penny; and the only fat thing he had was his belly, and no one knew how he managed to fill it, because he ate only a few cents' worth of bread, and yet he was rich as a pig; but that man, he had a mind that was a jewel (p. 308).

Thus, after being solicited to a flight of his imagination, the reader is quickly brought face to face with that reality for which he himself was yearning. It is an abrupt change of tone, which reveals the maturity of a writer who can produce great contrasts with unmatched skill. Even the language has suddenly changed. Whereas before it was imbued with a highly lyrical cadence, it now consists of spoken, down-to-earth, everyday intonations. The language of the rest of the story will be on the level of this second type of expressive pattern: not the highly lyrical, melodious lines of the contemplative opening paragraph, but the matter-of-factness of Mazzarò himself—and of those who have witnessed his rise and his fall.

Mazzarò was a self-made man. With grim determination and incessant work he had been able to rise from the level of poor laborer to the sphere of owner of immense lands and enormous herds. In his journey from rags to riches, he represents a common peasant myth and the personification of all the wildest dreams of the poor. Mazzarò was illiterate, but his mind was sharper than the Baron's, whose land he had swallowed up piece by piece. All he wanted was more and more property. Often he had difficulty tricking the local owners into selling their plots for almost nothing, but ultimately he was successful. "Four thousand mouths" fed on his land, and he was always among them, watching every detail. Yet he lived very sparingly, spending almost nothing on himself: "He didn't drink wine, he didn't smoke, he didn't take snuff, even though his fields along the river produced lots of tobacco . . . he didn't have the vice of gambling or of women" (p. 309). He was made for property, and property was made for him.

For a man like Mazzarò, only one kind of tragedy exists: the realization that he and his property are not one and the same thing after all—and that, therefore, he will have to be separated from it. His initial identification with his lands and his herds appeared to live mostly in the realm of the observer's imagination, but actually it was also the result of Mazzarò's own deception. At the end of his story he becomes unconsciously aware of the fact that he cannot become identified with his herds and his trees simply because they have a life of their own, and so the more he wants them inseparable from himself, the more they reveal their elusiveness. He is deeply grieved by the arrival of old age and by the knowledge that he must die very much like those who own nothing, and that he must leave his property where it is. He reduces himself to the point of being envious of those young men who have no property but can still live the long years ahead of them. For it is "an injustice of God" to have worn yourself out all your life to acquire property, and then "when you finally have it, and you want more, you have to leave it!" (p. 312).

So, when they told him that the time had come to leave his property and think of his soul, he staggered out into the courtyard like a madman, and went around killing his ducks and his turkeys with his stick, and screamed: "My property, come with me" (p. 313).

This demented effort to take his property along with him in death demonstrates that Mazzarò has failed to possess it, and that, in fact, he had begun to lose it at the very moment he was acquiring it. Thus Mazzarò may be viewed as the powerful example of a man who does not understand that land cannot be owned, for it is the mother of all creatures, and it belongs to all. As a result, he has alienated himself from life (he has rejected the love of women, as well as the possibilities of having children and grandchildren) so that he could devote all his energies to the god of riches. Now he is forced to discover that it is a false god; but it is too late. "La roba" remains one of the most impressive stories written by Verga, because it is filled with the modern sense of isolation and alienation. While offering us Mazzarò's obsessive drive, Verga also demonstrates how empty our dreams of great riches would be, were they to come true.

In the history of Verga's development, "La roba" is unusually significant, not only as an isolated narrative, but for its constituting a preview of the central theme of *Mastro-don Gesualdo*—a new and rather sophisticated Mazzarò, and the hero of the second novel of the *I Vinti* series. Although much more complex and human, Gesualdo too will be driven by an irresistible compulsion for riches, will be rejected by his property—as well as by his family—and finally will die in total isolation.

Rather a novelette than a short story, "Pane nero" (Black Bread) is the longest and the most elaborate of *Novelle rusticane*. The theme of the black bread of poverty permeates its every page, until it achieves a surprisingly cynical conclusion. At the death of Nanni, whose illness (malaria) has slowly consumed all the family's meager resources, three children and their old mother must find a way to survive: Santo, who can hardly take care of his own family; Lucia, a beautiful girl who cannot afford to hope for a husband because she has no dowry; Carmenio, a boy who has to go out and earn his own bread and butter. And no one seems in the position to support the old mother. Santo, who has a wife and many children, sometimes thinks that it would have been better if he had never married. This regret, which Verga typically uncovers in his character, is quickly utilized for an appealing flashback: the days when Santo fell in love with Rossa and everything looked so fascinating. Now both the fascination and the dreams are gone. Santo and Rossa must toil in the fields from morning to night, and then see the fogs of May come in and destroy the growing wheat and with it their hopes for the future. Bitter disappointment, the feeling of having worked in vain, and deepening poverty, breed such ill humor that husband and wife even come to blows; but they make peace and try to help each other for the sake of the children. They, says Verga, implicitly evoking the etymology of "to conjugate," are "like oxen tied to the same yoke." This is "marriage now" (p. 342).

Meanwhile, Carmenio finds a job as a shepherd, and eventually the mother—who can no longer be a burden on Santo's shoulders—goes to stay with him. Lucia resents living with Santo and Rossa and having to care for someone else's children without the benefit of a husband (p. 342). There is a young man, Pino who courts her, but he soon disappears to marry—"for the love of bread" (p. 341)—a crippled old woman who is rich. Lucia decides to become a maid in the house of Don Venerando, a wealthy old man with young whims, who begins to court her and to promise her a dowry. She is in love with the kitchen boy, Brasi, but he does not want to marry her because she has no dowry, and advises her to give in to Don Venerando and to accept his gifts. The girl finds the old man physically repugnant, but finally ends up in his bed. It also happens that one night, during a snowstorm, the mother dies in Carmenio's hut. The boy finds instinctive protection in peacefully letting his imagination travel back and forth along the lanes of his past for the entire night. The day after, Lucia, Santo, and Rossa arrive at the hut, and gather around the dead woman's bed. It is an unexpected family reunion. Lucia is clearly pregnant, and Santo is determined to give her a piece of his mind, but immediately quiets down when Rossa, who has seen Lucia's money and expensive jewelry, remarks that the old woman must be happy in heaven. Then she adds to Lucia: "Now Brasi will marry you for sure" (p. 358).

"Pane nero" abounds in beautiful passages: the courting of Rossa by Santo, and of Lucia by Pino; the moments of hope and disappointment in the wheatfields; and, best of all, the memorable night of the snow with the long interior monologue of Carmenio, escaping reality while keeping a vigil for his dead mother.[13] But what is particularly significant is how—contrary to what happens in *I Malavoglia*—in "Pane nero" the fear of poverty leads the characters to ignore all moral scruples as long as they can obtain material benefits. Brasi pushes Lucia into Don Venerando's arms, thus assuring himself some money; and as soon as this goal is achieved, he is ready to marry her, even though she is carrying the old man's child. Lucia seems to have learned from Pino that love does not mean much without money, and, therefore, in prostituting her emotional needs she sees some sort of fatality. Santo and Rossa almost admire her for having succeeded in attaining financial security.

More than in any of Verga's other works, in "Pane nero" all the characters' actions appear to be determined by the need to assure the necessities of physical survival. Verga has always underlined the extreme importance of economic factors; in "Pane nero" he stresses it with unprecedented emphasis, to the point of letting nearly everything else fall by the wayside. Not even in "La roba" is the god of riches so ruthless.

In the world of the poor, man and animal live together, each trying to survive at the expense of the other. This is the meaning of the great "Storia dell'asino di San Giuseppe" (Story of the St. Joseph Donkey). When the little animal is still a "colt," its owners must sell it because they need money to buy medicine for their boy, who is ill with malaria. Neli, the new owner, exploits the "colt" before and during the harvest; but as soon as he has made enough money to buy a mule—"which is better" (p. 321)—he sells it. Now the "colt" turns into a donkey, and its owner makes it pull the plough. The harvest goes bad and it must again be sold. Thus the donkey becomes the property of the cart-driver, who overworks it and beats it; and to those who say, "let the poor animal catch its breath," he answers: "With its hide I must fix my own" (p. 324). When the donkey cannot pull the heavy load any longer, it is the lime man's turn to buy it; and finally a poor widow with a sick boy is talked into spending most of her money to acquire it so that she can bring firewood to the market. But one day her boy is caught stealing wood and is given a workover by the field watchman. At night, in despair the widow breaks up a neighbor's fruit tree, and in the morning loads all the branches on the donkey's back and starts out for the market. But spent, the old donkey kneels in the middle of the road, slowly collapses, and dies. Now totally destitute, the widow thinks of her sick boy and mumbles: "Now what'll we do?" (p. 327). The cart-driver buys her wood for virtually nothing, and then kicks the carcass, which gives out the sound of a "broken drum" (p. 327).

Much of the story is written from the viewpoint of the donkey itself—which tends to emphasize the interdependence between man and animal. When a colt, it is joyful and full of life—just like young Ieli, who lived with the creatures of the earth, and the birds and the clouds of the sky. When it has to work hard to return its owner what it has cost, and more, it gives everything it can, even though tired and thirsty. In those moments it seems as if the entire countryside were made not for joy, but for pain:

Then he let his muzzle and his ears droop, like a full-grown donkey, his eyes lifeless, as if it were tired of looking at the vast white countryside which was clouded here and there with dust from the threshing floors and seemed made only to let you die of thirst and to make you trot around on the sheaves (p. 321).

Those closing words seem to be spoken by the donkey itself, which thereby becomes human in every respect. Like human beings, it was born to earn its food with the bitter sweat of its brow. Man exploits the animal without pity, for man has to think of his own survival; but then man, too, is exploited and persecuted, and finally destroyed . . . for man, too, is born to suffer—whether his hopes for an abundant harvest are obliterated, or a child who has been beaten up is in the grips of fever, and there is nothing left except the emptiness of despair.

"Storia dell'asino di San Giuseppe" is a restatement and a redevelopment of the theme of the gray donkey in "Rosso Malpelo." In this case, however, we know much more of the animal, and we feel closer to it. The interaction between man and animal is based on the suggestion that they are fundamentally similar, both beasts of burden, both victims of an implacable destiny. The Saint Joseph donkey may be viewed as an allegory, or at least as a counterpart, of mankind in general—toiling from morning to night without reason, until it collapses, exhausted, into death.

On the surface "Gli orfani" (The Orphans) develops a similar theme. Meno's second wife is dying, and the neighbors say: "Some men aren't lucky with wives, just as some people have no luck with animals" (p. 299). After she dies, Meno has only one way to remember and praise her:

She didn't want me to call the doctor nor to spend money and buy medicine. I'll never find another wife like that, believe me! . . . She didn't wash herself so she wouldn't dirty water. . . . And on top of all this she had brought a good dowry, stuff that was worth as much as gold! And I have to give all back because we didn't have children!" (pp. 301–302).

The wife is clearly viewed as an economic factor, and her death is mourned as the disappearance of such a [favorable] factor. This approach is immediately restated through the mention of the bereavement that has befallen another villager: "Look at poor Angela," says a neighbor, "first her husband died, then her oldest son, and now her donkey's dying too" (pp. 303–304). So Meno goes to Angela's to see if he can do anything. With the loss of her donkey, Angela is also left an orphan, bereaved and deprived of the main means of support. As to Meno, the sorrow for the death of his wife quickly subsides, as he is easily convinced to marry again—a woman of means, of course, who takes advantage of the situation to secure herself a husband. Then standing before Angela's dead donkey, he speaks the closing, perfectly consistent, lines: "Why don't you have the donkey skinned now? At least get the money for its hide" (p. 306).

What then in the "Storia dell'asino di San Giuseppe" was the profoundly compassionate interaction between man and animal, in

"Gli orfani" has been translated into a purely cynical interpretation of man's motivations in regards to himself. This is a stark world, in which no one has a real sense of loss and where everyone tries to profit whenever possible, without scruples and without yielding to emotions.

"Libertà" (Freedom) is ablaze with violence. Never has Verga written a piece so full of killing, and never has the spilling of blood been more futile. The story is intended to recreate, and to interpret, an actual riot that took place in Bronte—a town on the western slopes of Mount Etna—during Garibaldi's Sicilian campaign in 1860. With the arrival of the "liberating" army, the peasants and the poor of Bronte decide that the new "freedom" will bring both the elimination of the exploiting landowning class and the sharing in the ownership of the lands. Thus they embark upon an orgy of blood. After they have axed down and trampled upon all the rich people in town, they are overwhelmed by the thought of what they have done, and withdraw to their hovels in silence and fear. The following day a general marches his soldiers into Bronte, and as a beginning he has five or six people shot. The others are taken to the city jail, and only three years later are they finally tried and sentenced to long periods of hard labor.

"The Charcoal man, while they were handcuffing him again, stammered: 'Where are you taking me? to jail? why? I didn't even get a foot of land. And they had said there was freedom!' " (p. 373). These are the last words of the story. On the surface they may remind us of the end of "Jeli il pastore." Such a similarity, however, is only technical. There Ieli is deeply convinced of having travelled the road of justice and thereby having reestablished natural equilibrium; here the charcoal man considers himself innocent simply because he did not get any land. He cannot understand what "freedom" may mean, if it does not give him definite economic benefits.

"Libertà" must be ranked among the most disquieting of Verga's works; not because of the violence burning the first half of the story, but because of the narrator's approach to the problem of social progress. The fearless heroes of the first pages are soon transformed into frightened children at the mercy of the punishing general, and then into pictures of dejection wasting away in jail. As far as the town is concerned, it is soon back to normal. The two classes make peace. "The rich could not work their lands with their own hands, and the poor could not make a living without the rich" (p. 372). Thus

Verga asserts that there is a reason why a certain social order exists, and that this social order cannot be disrupted without everyone being the loser. Verga is now siding with the conservatives—and with the social pessimists. He has a great deal of understanding for the poor and for why they might want to initiate bloody revolts. But he cannot accept the subversion of the prevailing structures, both because the poor are not prepared to take over the responsibility and because the rich are necessary—the two social classes being, therefore, interdependent. This attitude explains the tone of the story, with its underlying disapproval of the uprising, and its sarcasm. It also explains why this time Verga cannot write in the language of his characters, but must resort to a bourgeois *koiné*, which reflects his own principles and his personal reactions to that bloody event. He would have been unable to anticipate that such losers as the peasants of Bronte would evolve into the more enlightened and less violent winners of a century later.[14]

Although most of them individually are quite good, the remaining six "Rustic Tales" do not measure up to the quality of those covered so far, especially if "Libertà" should be excluded. "Il reverendo" (The Reverend Father)—probably the most significant of the six—is concerned with an unscrupulous priest who has managed to acquire large land holdings. After the arrival of the Kingdom of Italy, he must give up many of those "temporal" privileges that have been allowing him to defraud his fellowmen. As a result, he complains that there is no longer justice in the world. "Il reverendo" is a small-time Mazzarò and prefigures Canon Lupi, one of the shrewdest characters of *Mastro-don Gesualdo*. Of some interest is Verga's insistence on the priest's greed—which must be viewed as an expression of anticlericalism—and a quick reference to the priest's bidding at a land auction, which will be later expanded in the second novel of the *I Vinti* series.

"Cos'è il re" (So Much for the King) hinges on the naïveté of a litter driver, who is called upon to fetch the queen and therefore feels that the king will help him out when in need. But then the king orders roads built, thereby causing the litter driver to fall into such poverty that he must sell his mules to pay the taxes. He has obviously collaborated with his own adverse destiny. In his helplessness, the undeveloped protagonist does not inspire much sympathy; he looks very much like a statue. And Verga's cynical approach turns an implicitly tragic human event into a farce.

"Don Licciu Papa" focuses on the theme of the impossibility for the poor to be treated justly. The rich are always right, and can perpetrate all kinds of abuses with impunity: "Justice exists only for those who have money to spend" (p. 278), says one of the protagonists.

In "I galantuomini" (Gentry) it is the well-to-do who lose everything and who fall into the grips of despair. Although forced to the same level as the poor, they feel they must keep a front of respectability. But at the same time the ever-present need for survival makes them renounce those moral standards that only the rich can afford. Again we are presented with the now familiar concept that conventional morality is possible only as long as a comfortable living is assured. "I galantuomini" contains the seeds of a much better story: its characters are all victims of crushing circumstances; the language is vivid and the style racy. It suggests the outline for a novel that was never written—for many seem to be the narrative ideas pressing on Verga's mind at once, all of them clamoring for a fuller development.

The theme of "Il mistero" (The Mystery Play) recalls some of the tales of elemental passion we have encountered in *Vita dei campi*. Again, jealousy prompts a man to kill one who has taken from him the affection of his woman. As in "Pentolaccia," the name of the female protagonist is Venera, and as in "Cavalleria rusticana," the murder is perpetrated during the Easter festivities. But the story lacks cohesiveness. Clearly Verga no longer believes in the intrinsic power of human passions, which he has replaced with the economic need for survival.

Dissonant with the rest of the book is "Di là dal mare" (Across the Sea), which concludes the series as inappropriately as "Il come, il quando ed il perché" concludes *Vita dei campi*. Two young lovers have a brief, torrid season in a faraway Sicilian retreat; they promise each other the Romantic "forever," but very soon they must separate and face an unexciting way of life that can neither be ignored nor changed. However, the story is also an inventory of the various locations in the Plain of Catania, where the characters of *Novelle rusticane* live their modest but harrowing dramas. In a sense "Di là dal mare" resembles "Fantasticheria," with the difference that now the characters are incidental, for the story concentrates on the couple's love affair—and it is written in the affected and exclamatory expressive modes that were typical of young Verga, as well as of the bourgeois writers of his time.

IV   Per le vie *(Through the Streets)*

Also published in 1883, this series of short stories is almost as different from *Novelle rusticane* as *Il marito de Elena* was from *I Malavoglia*. Even the parallelism of the two titles emphasizes this difference: *Per le vie* points to the vicissitudes in the lives of city people, and thereby it stands in clear opposition to *Novelle rusticane*. The new stories are set in Milan, where Verga has now been living for over ten years. The characters are no longer the poor he had known during his adolescence, but some of the more or less colorful inhabitants of the Lombard metropolis. After his "Sicilian" books, however, these Milanese stories look rather pale.[15] Verga is now testing a style which stands halfway between that of his "bourgeois" writings and that of *Novelle rusticane*. Again he is also determined to engage in an extended psychological analysis.

"Il bastione di Monforte" (The Monforte Rampart) is an introductory piece intended to provide an atmosphere for the other eleven stories. Its prose is soft and sentimental, mostly descriptive. While in *Vita dei campi* and in *I Malavoglia* Verga eliminates description and interiorizes external factors, in "Il bastione di Monforte" he lingers on those external factors *per se*.

But even in these Milanes tales, there are times when Verga makes an effort to focus almost exclusively on the inner world of his characters. "In Piazza della Scala" is a monologue by a cabman stationed in La Scala square. He has problems with his family, and finds it very difficult to make ends meet. He encounters only the rich. Even the man who preaches equality in the newspapers appears to be extremely well off. "Money," the cabman says, "that's all one needs in this world!" (p. 395). It is the philosophy of Verga's have-nots. The story itself would be very effective, were it not for the protagonist, who is barely sketched, a man who but mumbles in the square. Similar is "Al Veglione" (At the Masked Ball), which is based on the contrast between Pinella, the liquor peddler unceasingly looking for undrained bottles, and the wasteful rich.

Much better is "Il canarino del N. 15" (The Canary of No. 15). A poor crippled girl sitting by the window ends up by falling in love with a young man who passes by every day, and who, on the other hand, begins to court her sister, Gilda—who, in turn, falls for a rich suitor and moves out of the house. The young man comes visiting every day in the hope of finding Gilda back, while the crippled girl becomes more and more infatuated with him. Suddenly her condition worsens, and soon she is dead. Generally, "Il canarino" reminds us of the old *Storia di una capinera;* even the bird symbols in the respective titles suggest a similarity. But there are important differences, not the smallest of which can be found in the end of "Il canarino": the young man moves to a distant district of the city, and in the girl's home sorrow quickly abates. It leaves us with the feeling that time heals all wounds and people continue living, often without even remembering the sufferings of those who have disappeared into death. In 1885 Verga rewrote the story as a two-act play under the title of *In portineria* (The Porter's Lodgings), but then he accentuated its already considerable sentimentalism.

"Amore senza benda" (Love without Veils) is pervaded with the same moral pessimism that is prevalent in *Novelle rusticane*. Even its language often echoes Sicilian expressions. Sandrino takes a fancy to a ballerina, but she prefers a rich patron. Sandrino, however, finds some consolation in marrying the daughter of his landlord; the latter, in turn, meets the ballerina and marries her, who is unfaithful to her husband by taking none other than Sandrino as her lover. The rich old man dies without willing a penny to his wife, and she is quickly thrown out by Sandrino himself, who is thereby making sure that no one touches any of his wife's (and, consequently, of his own) inheritance. It is again the theme of the omnipotence of money and of its overpowering even the most intimate feelings. The story is loosely constructed, with too many interacting characters and too many ambitious drives.

"Semplice storia" (A Simple Tale) must be rated as one of the best pieces of *Per le vie*. It may remind us of parts of Flaubert's *Un coeur simple,* which preceded it by a few years—most probably without having been read by Verga. "Semplice storia" is concerned with a poor and unattractive governess who falls in love with a Southern Italian soldier. Because of him she loses her job, but manages to find employment in a silk mill at Monza, where his battalion has been transferred. She becomes seriously ill and must be confined to a hospital for over two months. Upon her return, she discovers that her soldier has another girl, yet she is satisfied with whatever crumbs of companionship she can get. But as soon as his term is completed, the soldier goes back to his faraway town, where his fiancée is waiting. The story is based on the contrast between the cynical soldier and the deeply affectionate and loving girl; it is precisely this contrast that underscores its touching reality. The most moving scene takes place at the railway station: almost no words are spoken, but the girl is full of warm feelings, while the soldier's thoughts fly toward his future. It reminds us of the end of "Primavera," but it is far more intense. It proves that now Verga can treat a common, Romantic theme in an austere, and yet sensitive, manner.

"L'osteria dei 'Buoni Amici' " (The "Good Friends" Inn) deals with a rich young man who becomes involved with slum dwellers and ends up in jail. In "Gelosia" (Jealousy) Carlotta lives with one man after another in the consciousness of her degradation, and in the conviction that life cannot be any different for her. They are both weak stories. Verga's effort to create an appropriate expressive medium for his Northern characters, often by mixing their Milanese idiom with obviously Florentine forms and rhythms, renders the language artificial. It is this unsuccessful effort that is mainly responsible for our not being able to place the *Per le vie* series on the same level as the Sicilian stories.

"Via Crucis" (The Calvary Road) follows the progressive decline of a girl from her encounter with her first lover to her becoming a street walker. Santina is undoubtedly the victim of society; it is, in fact, social prejudice that forces her into prostitution as her only means of survival. But the story is badly structured: Verga has too much to tell and yet is in a hurry to conclude. The title itself implies that he is driven by the desire to call attention to society's victims and intends to produce a polemical piece. But the result is no more than a bittersweet story, whose excessive sentimentalism excites neither compassion nor repulsion.

Much more convincing is "Conforti" (Consolation). Arlia has a very difficult life: all her children die prematurely, except a girl who becomes pregnant and must be married to her lover—who, on the other hand, wants a dowry. Arlia's husband makes very little money and looks for consolation at the tavern; Arlia herself runs from one house to the other to dress the ladies' hair for a few lire. Finally, the girl marries, Arlia's husband finds comfort in wine, and she escapes reality in brandy. "Conforti" is one of the most disheartening of Verga's works. It tells us that we can protect ourselves from the blows of destiny only by either stoic acceptance or by inability to think. There is nothing in the conclusion of "Conforti" that conjures up a feeling of "melancholic optimism," as Giulio Marzot strangely comments.[16] Arlia belongs to the large family of Verga's "Doomed."

In "Camerati" (Buddies) our author is preoccupied with the Socialist ideas already widespread in Northern Italy, and takes a polemical stance against them on the grounds that they complicate, rather than solve, current problems. Two veterans of a Risorgimento war meet again in civilian clothes. Malerba works on his farm, trying to wrest his daily bread from the soil; his friend, Gallorini, is a railroad employee who speaks of social rights. He sounds like an educated version of young 'Ntoni Malavoglia, although 'Ntoni was risking much more. Malerba does not offer an opinion, for he is not interested in politics but in what is to Verga a far more realistic and a far more pressing issue:

"You don't know anything about the way the world goes! if they have a demonstration and shout 'Long live this' and 'Death to that,' you don't know what to say. You don't understand what we need!"
And Malerba kept nodding yes.—He needed rain for the wheatfields now. This coming winter he needed a new roof for the stable (p. 460).

Verga's point is very clear in these concluding lines. We are reminded of the general contents of "Libertà," with its conviction that existing social structures cannot, and should not, be altered. But the story is again faulty. Indeed, it is two stories. The first offers the explosive fury of a battle and develops the naïve—yet solid—personality of Malerba; the second is no more than an appendix, intended to make a political point, but remaining strongly out-of-tune with the preceding pages.

"L'ultima giornata" (The Last Day) tells of the dejected wanderings of a destroyed man on the eve of his suicide—and of the reactions of the people who meet him and consider him a nuisance. Those who are having a good time, when told of the man's death, indulge in banal comments and cheap jokes. The pages presenting the isolation and despair of the anguished protagonist are of truly superior quality. Man lives alone and dies alone, Verga keeps repeating. But never yet had this theme been dealt with so directly as in "L'ultima giornata." The protagonist does not know anyone, is looked upon with suspicion by both men and animals, does not have a name, is always referred to as "the stranger." Interestingly enough, "L'ultima giornata" concludes the *Per le vie* series, as if to imply that the other characters too are in the last analysis like this "stranger": all stranded in a world of egotism and alienation.

V Drammi intimi *(Personal Dramas)*

The slim volume with only six stories, and published after *Novelle rusticane* and *Per le vie*, looks more like a series of literary exercises than the fruit of profound commitment. In subject matter it is rather heterogeneous—journeying from the love affairs of refined aristocrats who have nothing to do except seek diversions for their excessively sharpened sensitivity, to the sad existence of those who are persecuted by destiny across the Lombard plains, and finally to the administration of Sicilian justice after a senseless killing. All the stories are readable, but none is of high quality.

"Drammi ignoti" (Unknown Dramas), later retitled "Dramma intimo" (Personal Drama), tells the story of a rich lady (Countess Orlandi), who has a lover (Marquis Roberto Danei), and who soon discovers that her ailing daughter is suffering because she has fallen deeply in love with him. To save her, she convinces Roberto to marry her daughter, and she herself retires into resigned solitude, becomes ill, and dies. It is an openly Romantic tale in which the two main characters exchange their destinies. Conceivably, it was originally intended as a chapter of *Eros*. The striking similarity in the names of the characters seems to corroborate this impression. If so, we must admit that Verga has managed to rewrite his expunged episode so well that it reads better than the novel. The plot itself resembles, at least in spirit, "Il come, il quando ed il perché."

In "L'ultima volta" (The Last Time) a lover pays his last visit to his dying mistress: as he exits her room, he meets her husband. There are two widely different versions of this story. The second (later renamed "L'ultima visita" [The Last Visit]) is the more successful. Neither one, however, spares us a feeling of boredom. Of still lower quality is "Bollettino sanitario" (Medical Bulletin), in which a man who is ill with tuberculosis begins a passionate correspondence with his ex-mistress, who promises to come back to him, until—having observed him in incognito—she pronounces herself dead. Everything seems to imply that love is nothing but a figment of the imagination—an expression of vanity, egotism, and hypocrisy.

"Tentazione" (Temptation) is much better. After a pleasant afternoon, three Milanese young men, almost without realizing what

they are doing, rape and kill a girl they happen to meet in the
outskirts of the city. The thesis is that the most important events in
life are produced by chance and that one has absolutely no control
not only over them, but over the actions they elicit. "La Barberina
di Marcantonio" (Marcantonio's Little Barbara) tells of a miller who
loses two wives and all of his children except Barberina—who, however, ends up by dying in the mill house during a storm. The best
piece in the series, "La chiave d'oro" (The Gold Key), is set in Sicily.
One evening the canon priest's field watchman kills a man for stealing some olives. The priest is only worried about himself and the
trouble such an incident may bring him. Soon he manages to corrupt the pretrial judge with a succulent dinner and a new gold key
for his watch. The piece is woven on two polemical threads: the
greed of priests and the venality of those who are charged with the
administration of justice. The first was central to "Il reverendo" and
will soon be re-presented with great power in *Mastro-don Gesualdo;*
and the second constituted the theme of "Don Licciu Papa," where
it became epitomized in the aphorism, "Justice exists only for those
who have money to spend." But now Verga's attitude is one of
profound cynicism, which causes the story to be so excessively compressed that it reads almost like an outline, cold and caustic.

Verga never reprinted *Drammi intimi* as such. Three of the stories
were included in the 1891 *I ricordi del capitano D'Arce* (Captain
D'Arce's Recollections)—two of them with slightly different titles.
The other three were abandoned, until Lina and Vito Perroni reprinted them in the appendix of their 1942 edition of *Tutte le
novelle.*

VI Vagabondaggio *(Wanderers)*

It was published in 1887, and brought together a number of narratives that had been written during the previous three years. The
first of them, which lends its title to the volume, is the longest and
possibly the best. It centers around Nanni, a boy who grows up in a
world of adults. One day he leaves his father together with a little
girl, whom he soon abandons in order to obtain a job. He becomes
an assistant to a quack doctor, until he is forced to return to the town
of his origin, where he discovers that his father has died. Nanni
decides to marry a well-to-do girl, whom no one wants because of
her loose morals. He is now an adult, for he understands the
significance of financial security and the irrelevance of all traditional

concerns about sexual mores. "Vagabondaggio" is a complex story that appears to be woven on many of Verga's previous themes. There are parts which are reminiscent of "Cavalleria rusticana," "Jeli il pastore," and "Pane nero." Don Tinu, the cloth peddler, speaks like Alfio; the pages devoted to Nanni and the little girl Grazia are strikingly similar to those evoking the boy Ieli as he discovers the natural wonders with little Mara, and as Nanni grows up he becomes an amalgamation of Pino and Brasi. The fact that, like the stories of *Vita dei campi* and *Novelle rusticane*, "Vagabondaggio" is set in the Plain of Catania, may explain some of these similarities. The style is rapid and dense—and free of unnecessary descriptions. Particularly important is Verga's philosophy as it springs from the characters' lips. "The world is large," says Tinu, "and everyone must mind his own business" (p. 33)[17]—a purely opportunistic philosophy that places man on a rather elementary moral level and in contradiction with more civilized standards.

Also interesting in "Vagabondaggio" is its pervasive sense of human solitude. Man is totally alone and must be able to satisfy his own needs without ever expecting help from others. There is no group, not even the family, to which one can turn. But while dwelling on the theme of human isolation, Verga also discovers inside the characters the related theme of man's need to obey his nomadic instinct. Nanni's wanderings afford the writer the opportunity of creating some rather beautiful passages, even though they are soon stifled by practical solutions. At the end, as Nanni reflects upon those who must keep toiling for their subsistence, he exclaims: "Poor devils! They still have to go about the world to earn their bread!" (p. 41). This summarizes the meaning of the work. For whoever leads a wanderer's life does so only because he has to. If he has an opportunity to settle down in comfort and without any further worries, he takes it. Thereby a story that at first promised to be a presentation of the alternating fortunes of the wanderer, is translated into the detached commentary of one who is finally free of all survival problems and can appreciate bourgeois security. Thus by clinging to the objectivity of human realities, Verga deromanticizes a common Romantic motif.

A similar theme lies at the foundation of "Artisti da strapazzo" (Drifting Artists), with its third-rate singers travelling the provinces in the inexhaustible hope of finding jobs in local cafés. The protagonist, a girl who has lost her voice, is desperately in love, first with a baritone who soon abandons her, and then with a maestro to whom she cannot give herself. Destiny moves the characters from one place to another. Even when it allows them to remain in the same town for a short period of time, it still has them wait a telegram announcing their departure. If some of them change jobs, ironically the new occupations force them to keep wandering from town to town.

In reference to "Vagabondaggio" and to "Artisti da strapazzo," Luigi Russo observes: "With more artistic concentration and with the further development of similar themes, Verga could have given us a new and original conception of both art and the human condition. He would have no longer remained only the poet of generous primitivism, as in *Vita dei campi*, or of the religion of the family hearth, as in *I Malavoglia*, or of the melancholy greed for material possessions, as in *Novelle rusticane*, or of the sadness of the poor wretches peopling his Milanese stories, but he would have also been the poet of the desolate wanderers, of those who have no past and no future . . . and can find no more than incidental solace to their lives."[18]

"Un processo" (A Trial) speaks of a man (Malannata) who has killed Rosario Testa for persisting in going with his mistress, a public woman. Malannata, never jealous of her other men, could not tolerate Rosario, from whom she seemed to receive very special gratification. Two passages stand out in the story: the mistress's testimony, an extraordinarily frank statement that contrasts sharply with the hypocrisy of the district attorney, the judge, and the jurors; and the final confession of the accused, who bares his deepest feelings in a truly memorable soliloquy.

In "Il segno d'amore" (The Mark of Love) a man cannot accept being rejected by the woman he loves, in favor of a rival. Finally he slashes her face, producing a disfiguration that will give her reason to remember one who has loved her. In "Il bell'Armando" (Handsome Armand) a woman has a lover who spends all her money, jilts her and goes on to marry a young girl. The woman attempts to kill her ex-lover and earns life imprisonment. Because of their sexually motivated violence, these last three stories are reminiscent of *Vita dei campi*, but they do not carry the same emotional impact.

"Nanni Volpe" may be viewed as a rewriting of "La roba," even though it does not possess the depth and the breadth of that famed story. Nanni is a small-time Mazzarò who has made a great deal of money; but in contrast to Mazzarò, and somewhat late in life, he marries a young woman, who immediately engages in an affair with his nephew. Nanni knows, but says nothing. He tells his wife that he has willed her his entire estate, and to his nephew he tells the same thing. Thus he, taken ill with malaria, is treated like a king by both of them. When he dies, they discover that he has willed his estate to the hospital. Such posthumous revenge may indicate that the writer is indulging in an unexpected taste for jest. Nanni Volpe, in fact, may remind us of classical situations, such as Boccaccio's Ciappelletto, who manages to fool everyone, even after death. "Nanni Volpe" is tightly knit, but its sarcasm rebuffs any possibility for the refreshing cathartic laughter issuing from the great Decameronian story.

Violence born of peasant superstition erupts in "Quelli del colera" (Cholera Times), a hair-raising tale of how fear of death causes the villagers to murder innocent people. The narration is rather homogeneous, but it is again marred by the author's cynicism. Also imbued with cynicism are "La festa dei morti" (All Soul's Day) and "L'agonia di un villaggio" (The Agony of a Village), as well as ". . . E chi vive si dà pace" (Let the Dead Bury the Dead), in itself a good piece that should be included with the Milanese stories of *Per le vie*, and whose title, however, points at Verga's belief that human feelings are strictly dependent upon self-interest and personal gratification. As a last resort, to convince her fiancé that she has completely forgotten her previous lover, a girl produces his death certificate; but even this leaves her fiancé indifferent. The irony pervading the closing pages destroys the occasional tenderness of the others. A similar tone permeates "Il maestro dei ragazzi" (The Teacher)—the long and delicate story of the daydreams of a schoolteacher who meets with bitter disappointment when he discovers the unremitting egotism of his fellow villagers. In the closing piece, "Lacrymae rerum" (The Tears of Things), a house shares in its inhabitants' misery until the last one of them disappears and the house itself falls under the picks of the wreckers. This time our author indulges in sentimentalism.

Vagabondaggio is the book of Verga's bitter and disillusioned contemplation of his fellow human beings—or, perhaps more likely, it is the product of a writer too far removed from his characters to be capable of looking at them with compassionate eyes. The reader may be tempted to conclude that, having seemingly lost confidence in life, Verga cannot continue writing much longer. Indeed, he appears to be repeating himself. But in retrospect it must be recognized that what looks like repetition in reality constitutes a persistent search for a new approach to human actions and motivations. Verga is, in fact, about to produce his last masterpiece.

CHAPTER 5

Mastro-don Gesualdo

A S noted at the beginning of Chapter 3, the definitive title of the second novel of the *I Vinti* series was first mentioned in a letter to Salvatore Paola on April 21, 1878, and repeated in the preface to *I Malavoglia* with appropriate explanations: "In *I Malavoglia* it is still only the struggle for material needs. Once these are satisfied," the search for economic well-being "will turn into greed for riches, and will be embodied in a middle-class character, *Mastro-don Gesualdo. . . .*" The new novel was to be written almost immediately after the prose-poem of Master 'Ntoni, but Verga postponed it to devote himself to the composition of many shorter narratives and to the consideration of a vast number of characters. Those narratives served as excursions through several expressive levels, and thus they helped to broaden the experience of *I Malavoglia*. For *Mastro-don Gesualdo* Verga needed to be in full possession of the expressive mediums of the common people, of the wasted but still proud aristocracy, and particularly of the Sicilian bourgeoisie. The difficulty of assimilating the three idioms and of creating from them a new, original and most fitting language for his characters, may explain why he had to postpone the composition of the novel.

Finally, between July 1 and December 16, 1888, *Mastro-don Gesualdo* was serialized in the prestigious literary journal *Nuova Antologia*. There is reason to believe that Verga began publishing the novel well before he had completed it. In fact, as the last installment appeared in print, he soon began to rewrite it in its entirety, with the result that, while the first chapters remained almost the same in the final version as in the *Nuova Antologia* draft, the rest of the novel was completely transformed—with fundamental alterations involving not only the structure and the style, but also the very personalities of the characters. The 1888 second half sounds like a series of undeveloped sketches, jotted down in a hurry, while

127

the final version, published by Emilio Treves at the end of 1889, is
structurally quite well balanced. Verga's success in turning a fairly
approximate narration into what is generally considered a masterpiece during such a short period of time, is in itself cause for
amazement. It is most probable that he kept reworking his text on
the Treves proofs until the very day the last sheet was printed. In
fact, the manuscript he sent to his publisher (now owned by Treves's
successor, Livio Garzanti) is again substantially at variance with the
printed 1889 version. In addition to many occasional stylistic im-
provements, some of the most celebrated passages, including the
last page, are missing—thereby strongly suggesting that Verga did
indeed keep changing and amplifying his text while he was correct-
ing the printer's proofs.[1]

Mastro-don Gesualdo is the epic of the economic compulsion
relentlessly driving a man toward the acquisition of greater and
greater wealth and toward the power that such wealth generates.
Throughout his previous works Verga had regularly stressed the
significance of financial well-being and of how its presence, or its
absence, conditions all other aspects of human life. Now he pulls
together all those considerations and observations to fuse them into
a new and vigorous unity. Greed for riches obsesses nearly everyone
of the numerous characters in the novel—yet only the protagonist,
Gesualdo, rises above the pettiness and the abjection of the others.
He wants wealth; yet he does not conceive of it as an end unto itself,
but rather as a means to power: the power to realize many other
aspirations—such as that of reaching the top of the social ladder and
dominating an entire town. The philosophy standing as a motivating
force behind the novel may be found summarized in two familiar-
sounding aphorisms: "The world belongs to those who have money"
(p. 64[2]), and "Everyone works in his own interest" (p. 161). But
even though Gesualdo's plans and actions are in harmony with these
principles, he never appears narrow-minded or narrowly self-centered. "His own interest" often may signify also the interest of many
other people; yet the philosophy that brings him success carries
within itself the seeds of his destruction. Unlike Mazzarò, Gesualdo
is not satisfied with money and land: he wants respectability, which
he believes he can attain by marrying into the town aristocracy. It
will be precisely this vanity—a new and different kind of greed—
that will cause him to lose everything to the equally greedy, aristocratic son-in-law, and to die alone. Yet, throughout the novel both

the town and every one of its inhabitants exist only as a function of Gesualdo. But when he himself is vanquished, his defeat is born of the power he exerts on his environment and not of anyone's actions.

The ironic double epithet—*mastro-don*—refers to the standing of Gesualdo Motta—the name of a commoner—in the society of Vizzini (the Sicilian town where most of the action takes place). *Mastro* defines an independent workman, a skilled laborer, or—as is our case—a mason; a *don*, on the other hand, is a member of the landowning gentry. Mastro-don, therefore, gives us at once the past and the present of the protagonist, his roots in the working class as well as his claims to the aristocratic level. But, more importantly, it points out the attitude of the townsfolk. As Verga himself wrote to Edouard Rod, "*Mastro-don* is the sarcastic nickname pinned by the town's backbiters on the lowly laborer who has become wealthy."[3] We must add that it also stresses the power of Gesualdo's personality over all those who delude themselves in belittling him.

I *The Events*

The action of the novel spans from before 1820 to 1850—two dates vaguely corresponding to the political uprisings referred to in the course of the narration. An additional date to keep in mind is 1837, when Sicily was hit by a severe cholera epidemic. Like *I Malavoglia,* the novel begins *in medias res,* without descriptions, without hesitations, and without waste of words. Now Verga even avoids introducing his major characters; yet they are all immediately present.

Early one morning the old palace of the Traos—Don Diego, his brother Don Ferdinando, and their frail sister, Bianca—the most aristocratic, but also the poorest, family in town—is ablaze. Fearing for his own house, a neighbor, Gesualdo Motta, takes up the leadership in an effort to extinguish the fire. In the general confusion, Don Diego enters his sister's bedroom and there he discovers their second cousin, Baron Ninì Rubiera. Bianca is seized by a fit of convulsions. A doctor ascertains that she is pregnant. The first chapter, filled with movement and drama, quickly establishes a solid basis for the action of the entire novel. Gesualdo offers a rather accurate image of himself as a man of action who has no time to waste.

The following day Don Diego attempts to arrange an urgent marriage between Bianca and Ninì. But Ninì's mother, the wealthy Baroness Rubiera, refuses her consent simply because the girl is

poor. "What has Bianca gotten into her head?" she shouts. "Does
she think she will become the Baroness Rubiera?" (p. 35). Don
Diego may speak of honor, of social obligations, of the fact that
Bianca was born in a noble family, but the baroness understands
everything in terms of money. "My ancestors," she adds, "who
made my son a Baron . . . do you know who they were? People who
hoed the soil! . . . with the sweat of their brow, d'you understand?
They did not kill themselves working to let their property fall into
anybody's hands, d'you understand?" (pp. 35–36). And then she
concludes with cruel clarity: "I want my son to marry a good dowry"
(p. 36). Don Diego does not understand, and staggers back home
without being able to say another word. Baroness Rubiera immediately reveals herself as the female counterpart of Mastro-don
Gesualdo, even though she will prove more narrow-minded.
Meanwhile, we begin to perceive who the real victims of the fire
are: not the palace, but the people, including Mastro-don Gesualdo
himself.

With the help of the master intriguer Canon-priest Lupi, Baroness Rubiera sets in motion the marriage machine: her son must we.¹
Fifi Margarone; and Bianca Trao, Mastro-don Gesualdo. With the
ruthlessness of those who seek exclusively their personal advantage,
they make all the overtures the same evening, at a party, where
Bianca herself overhears the negotiations. Gesualdo is receptive to
Canon Lupi's proposition, thus indicating a serious interest in entering the aristocratic ruling class; yet, deep down, he knows that he
cannot become one of them.

At this moment, Verga dwells on the presentation of a full day in
his protagonist's life, thereby sharpening his image. Gesualdo is
busy running from one place to another to keep everything well in
hand and to supervise his workers, without resting for a minute,
without even taking the time for a quick meal. He deeply believes in
work and in the building and the augmentation of his personal fortune. But there is another side to his personality. He lives with a
totally devoted housekeeper, Diodata, the only person with whom
he finds peace and contentment. She has given him two children,
but she realizes that social laws will not allow him to marry her.
Gesualdo can no longer marry just any woman, and so much less one
of Diodata's condition, as he himself tells her: "A man can't always
do what he likes. I am no longer as free as when I was a poor devil
with nothing" (p. 85). The god of wealth chooses his victims pre-

cisely among the wealthy. Diodata is aware of this; she knows the rules governing society; like Mena Malavoglia, she is willing to accept her destiny. And, as is to be expected, there is a man, Nanni l'Orbo, ready to marry her for the sake of the dowry Gesualdo is providing.

Although the Trao brothers are opposed to the marriage of their sister to Mastro-don Gesualdo, Bianca realizes that she has no other choice. The wedding is not joyous. The two brothers refuse to attend (the descendants of a king cannot let their sister marry a common worker), and so does most of the aristocracy in town. Then, in the bridal chamber, Bianca tries to tell Gesualdo her secret, but cannot carry through, and submits to him without love. The wedding night is one of the high points of the novel. The delicate and, for his times, scabrous subject is treated by Verga with a few masterful strokes that suggest the underlying tragedy without indulging in sentimental effusiveness. To preserve and expand the power of money, Don Gesualdo has given up his devoted companion, Diodata, and has found himself involved in marriage with a total stranger.

The second part of the novel begins with Gesualdo purchasing vast land holdings at the city's auction. His being able to vanquish all the bids of the patricians enrages both the wealthy and the poor. There is an uprising, and Don Gesualdo is forced to seek shelter in Diodata's home. Her husband, Nanni l'Orbo, promptly accuses him of having seduced her and blackmails him into relinquishing a piece of land in reparation. The same evening Bianca's brother Diego dies, and Bianca, who had rushed to his deathbed, "prematurely" gives birth to a daughter exactly in the same place where the child had been conceived.

Now Verga's attention turns to the father of Bianca's little girl for the purpose of proving how the noblemen of Vizzini are trapped by Don Gesualdo. Ninì Rubiera falls madly in love with a vaudeville actress and, since his mother does not let him touch a cent, he asks Don Gesualdo for a large loan to be utilized to win the woman. Gesualdo is very happy to oblige, for he is certain that such a loan, plus the accrued interest, will eventually produce a substantial piece of property. Soon gossip brings the transaction to the attention of Baroness Rubiera. She threatens to disinherit Ninì, but she has a seizure that leaves her paralyzed and unable to speak. Ninì's fiancée (Fifì Margarone) breaks the engagement in an uproar that involves many families. At the end of the chapter we find Baron Ninì Rubiera administering his mother's property with considerable passion—and totally oblivious of his mistress. We again realize that for Verga's people money and property constitute the only true deities.

At this point it must be noted that in the first version of the novel jealousy was Gesualdo's motivation for lending money to Baron Rubiera. He was determined to avenge himself for the young man's affair with Bianca in the only way he knew: by slowly appropriating his lands. In the definitive edition, Gesualdo is interested on one side in acquiring the property and on the other in outwitting his aristocratic competitor. As to Bianca's premarital affair with the Baron and the true paternity of the baby girl, Gesualdo never finds out. We must also insist that, in spite of its corrections and changes, the second half of part two remains weak and drawn out, and it constitutes one of the reasons why *Mastro-don Gesualdo* cannot be placed on the same artistic level as *I Malavoglia*.

With part three we are again in the mainstream of the story. The little daughter has been baptized as Isabella. At the age of five she is sent to a boarding school in Palermo, where she associates with the proud daughters of the Sicilian nobility, and when Gesualdo comes to see her, she is ashamed of his way of dressing and his rough hands—so much so that she has herself called Isabella Trao. Soon everyone at school calls Gesualdo Trao too. He lavishes Isabella with presents of all sorts, thereby defeating, through her, his aristocratic competitors. In the meantime, Ninì Rubiera's debt to Gesualdo has grown tremendously, and the baron is forced to marry an old maid for her dowry. Gesualdo automatically acquires some first-rate land, which—as he himself remarks—will someday be Isabella's dowry. It is another piece of irony: Ninì Rubiera, the actual father, becomes the one to supply the girl's dowry. Verga never forgets how destiny interweaves the threads of human lives according to its own peculiar laws of justice.

A disastrous cholera epidemic sweeps through Sicily. Gesualdo provides food and shelter to whomever is in need. As his own guests in a large villa he accepts Bianca's cousin, Donna Cirmena, and her young nephew, Corrado La Gurna. Isabella too returns from Palermo, but does not like the quiet of the countryside. To while away the hours of boredom, she listens to Corrado's poetry and quickly falls in love with its author. Cirmena encourages the affair, for she would like her nephew to become heir to Gesualdo's vast fortune. Gesualdo becomes aware of the development and asks Bianca to watch over her daughter. But Bianca has no strength. She too is now ill—not with cholera, but with consumption, the disease that has destroyed her family, and which in Verga represents the deterministic result of aristocratic inbreeding. Concurrently, Gesualdo's father, Nunzio, dies of malaria, surrounded by insensitivity and egotism, just as will happen to Gesualdo himself. After the usual screaming and tearing of hair, Gesualdo's sister asks him for her share of all of his possessions—for they ostensibly belong to the entire family, now that their father is dead. Gesualdo is deeply shocked and leaves, his back bent in sadness. But we are reminded that greed keeps motivating most of our characters, often driving them to unexpected extremes. In fact, if one has amassed a fortune by the sweat of his brow and the loss of his sleep, the others—his friends and relatives—will only hate him for it, and will demand a share of that fortune—for nothing!

As the cholera ends, Gesualdo is busy keeping an eye out for Corrado La Gurna and his daughter. Finally he puts Isabella in a convent, but, through the complicity of Cirmena, Isabella elopes with Corrado. Rather than recognizing the *fait accompli*, Gesualdo has Corrado arrested and then agrees to arrange a wedding between Isabella and the Duke of Leyra from Palermo, who bears a highly illustrious family name, but needs the girl's dowry. Isabella wants Corrado, but now everyone concedes that if the father does not give her any money she cannot marry the boy, who is poor. She is told that love may be a good thing, but without money it disappears very fast, while it is easy to become used to any husband, if he is rich. This is familiar philosophy, which Isabella herself acknowledges as valid.

The wedding of convenience arranged by Gesualdo for his daughter has extraordinary parallels in the novel, all of them intended to insist on the morality—or immorality—rooted in social pretenses. Like her mother, Isabella has had an affair with a second cousin, and like her mother, she is pregnant (as it will be later implied); unlike her mother, however, she will continue her affair after she is married. But like her mother, she is forced by money considerations to renounce the man she loves and to accept as husband a man who will remain a total stranger to her. Still more significant is another set of coincidences. Gesualdo has arranged a marriage between his still young mistress and Nanni l'Orbo, who was motivated exclu-

sively by "arid and self-centered greed," for his passion for money
was "purely primitive and amoral."[4] The Duke of Leyra is different
only because he appears more outwardly refined. He wants money,
and to get it he agrees to marrying someone else's mistress; he
exploits every circumstance to get more of it, including threatening
to separate from his wife and seeing to it that Gesualdo dies without
a will, so that his wife—and consequently himself—inherits all the
vast fortune. With these key episodes Verga is suggesting that peasants and dukes are equally abject and basely greedy; if there is a
difference, it is one of appearance, not of substance.

As the novel progresses, Gesualdo's complex and somewhat rigid
personality is forced to relax and mellow by the blows of a destiny he
himself has fashioned. He had always nurtured tender feelings for
Isabella. Even preventing her from marrying Corrado La Gurna
derived from his intense desire for her to have a splendid life. But
all this was an error, and he seems to have become aware of it.
Although he blames Cirmena and Corrado for what has happened,
behind his words we perceive a measure of regret for having pushed
events along a path that can no longer be altered. Now Gesualdo
hears of constant fights between Isabella and her husband, that the
duke is resentful because his wife has had a child so soon and wants
to separate. While feeling disgraced, Gesualdo tries to patch things
up with his son-in-law by disbursing large sums of money.

It would not be an exaggeration to state that part four of the novel
is presided over by the dark deity of death. Bianca is rapidly wasting
away, and while he is cognizant of how serious the disease is,
Gesualdo keeps hoping that some day she will suddenly recover. He
remains constantly at home, looking for a glimpse of improvement,
and spending as much money as he can for doctors and medicines.
He avoids speculations; he even neglects his lands and his contracts.
There is another revolution, with the peasants claiming their share
of the public lands. The rich want to plot with Gesualdo, but he
insists that he does not care, that his own revolution is right there, at
home. In the midst of all the petty greed, Gesualdo reveals himself
as the only really noble character in the book. Verga has endowed
him with a compulsive drive for riches, but he has refused to make
him sordidly avaricious. Around him, under Bianca's very eyes,
there are those who are already scheming to take advantage of his
money by selecting a second wife for him. But he, crushed by
Bianca's condition and his own helplessness, cannot even fathom
such maneuvers.

With the pretext of the so-called revolution, and for the purpose of trapping Don Gesualdo, one of the small-time politicians in town kills Nanni l'Orbo, Diodata's husband, while she was trying to assist the dying Bianca. Gesualdo does not seem to care about this attempt at framing him either. Soon Bianca dies without Isabella having come to see her. Don Gesualdo, alone, begins to cry like a child. On the street people accuse him of all kinds of abuses; a few come to talk to him, a matron goes so far as to propose that he marry her daughter. He cannot believe his ears. He is old and he knows that he is very ill. "With his mouth always bitter, he had lost appetite and sleep; he had cramps in his stomach, like mad dogs biting inside him" (p. 335).

There is another riot in town, with the poor again wanting their share. The crowd moves toward Gesualdo's warehouses, and toward his home. They are all against him—all ready to attack the man who is doomed, to snatch from him whatever he may still have. The crowd is incited against Gesualdo by the well-to-do, who are planning to save their own property at his expense. He finds shelter in the dilapidated Trao palace, which is still occupied by Ferdinando—looking like the ghost of himself. Gesualdo in his fever sees "Bianca, Diodata, Master Nunzio, and still others, who pass before his clouded eyes, and then another himself, slaving and toiling in the sun and in the wind. And all of them, surly, spit into his face such words as 'Jackass! Jackass! what have you done? It serves you right!' " (p. 352). When he returns home he discovers that his sister has moved in and behaves like the real mistress of the house.

Finally Gesualdo agrees to be examined by a group of specialists. They diagnose cancer of the stomach. The old man manages to have himself transferred to one of his country estates, but "once there among his possessions, he realized that it was all over, that there was no hope, for he did not care about that property of his any longer" (p. 362). Gesualdo had been wanting to acquire property, and once he had managed to acquire it he had identified with it. All his mistakes had stemmed from his overestimating the significance of wealth, never from underestimating it. Now that he is completely alone—even more so than before he had a wife and a "daughter"— his property, his land, would be the only reality left. Yet he does not care. Meanwhile, he cannot understand why he must die when the rest of the world goes on living, and therefore he decides that his possessions must share his own destiny. Like a madman he staggers about killing his hens and his turkeys, destroying the tree buds and

the young wheat. It is the same demented despair that had overcome Mazzarò at the end of "La roba."

As soon as he is informed of his father-in-law's condition, the
Duke of Leyra comes from Palermo, takes full charge of the old
man, and has him brought to his own palace, where he can watch
him in case he should want to write a will. The scene of Gesualdo's
departure from his country estate is full of pathos. Of all his friends,
only Diodata is standing in the street to say good-bye. " 'Ah!
Diodata. . . . Did you come to wish me a good trip?', he said. She
nodded yes, yes, her eyes filling with tears. 'Poor Diodata! you are
the only one to remember your master.' . . . Slowly she drew back
from the litter, reluctantly, and went back to the house, stopping on
the threshold, humble and very sad" (p. 364). Thus the devoted
creature who had given Gesualdo his rare moments of happiness,
disappears from the novel.

The closing chapter has often been hailed as one of the peaks in
Verga's career.[5] Gesualdo is now in the great palace of Palermo, in a
world he does not understand, far away from his fields and from the
noisy streets of his town. His son-in-law and his daughter have given
him a little apartment upstairs. But he soon discovers that this world
is made up of superficiality, of egotism, of duplicity, and of waste-
fulness. He spends much time reminiscing. But what especially
grieves him is the thought of all the money being squandered in the
palace, of his property that is both neglected and devoured. He
would like to talk to his daughter, but she pays him hurried visits.
He knows that she is not happy in that house either, and from her
quarrels with her husband he learns that she has a lover. Doctors
come to see him, but they treat him like an object, without listening
to what he has to say. He wants to dictate a will, but the duke keeps
saying that it is premature, adding that it is not necessary after
all—Isabella being an only child. Finally Gesualdo decides to have a
frank talk with his daughter. In an unforgettable moment, he ex-
tends his arms toward her for the last time, and says: "Let us talk
business" (p. 379); she denies that they should, but he insists:
"There are important questions to discuss. I cannot afford to waste
time" (p. 379). So he begins to speak of those beautiful lands that she
should treasure, and adds that he would like to leave a small fraction
of his property to some people toward whom he feels he has an
obligation—obviously the children Diodata had borne him. But
Isabella is not listening. They are two irreconcilable worlds.

Gesualdo is truly alone. Even the person in whom he had always thought he could find some degree of understanding was revealing herself distant and hostile. Now, from the depth of his isolation and total powerlessness, Gesualdo is able to face death with full detachment from all he leaves behind—not as a moment of destruction, but as one of liberation. It is in this spirit that he pronounces his last words: "Now . . . I want to clear my accounts with God" (p. 381). Thus, with the resoluteness and the practicality of his business past, he is accepting destiny's last call.

One early morning, as Gesualdo is being watched over with growing annoyance by one of the servants, death comes. Soon the room is full of people, joking and talking inanities, as if they had finally been freed of a heavy burden. Even before the great abyss of death, their own petty egotism prevails. And we are left with the feeling of having witnessed the end of an existence that was misdirected, of a myth that had to collapse.

II   *Concluding Observations*

At the beginning of part three, Gesualdo surveys his human condition, while unconsciously attempting to uncover the reasons for his failures. But he cannot see beyond self-serving rationalizations.

. . . Bianca did not seem as if she would give him any other heirs. After the baby was born, she had never recovered; as a matter of fact, she was declining from day to day, herself gnawed by the same worm that had eaten up all the Traos, and it was certain that she would not have any more children. A true punishment of God. A bad bargain—although he was careful not to complain, not even with the canon-priest Lupi, who had first proposed it. When you have made a blunder, you'd better keep quiet and not talk about it, so as not to let your enemies have the upper hand. Nothing, nothing had that marriage brought him; neither dowry, nor male child, nor the new relatives' help, nor even what Diodata used to give him: a moment of relaxation, an hour of pleasantness, like a glass of wine to a poor man who has toiled all day! Not even that! A wife who went sour between your hands, who froze your caresses, with that face and those eyes, with her being frightened, as if you were making her fall into mortal sin, each time. . . . It was the blood of her race that refused. You can't graft peaches on an olive tree. . . . But he wasn't taken in, no. True, he was a peasant, but he was as sharp as a peasant too. And he had his own pride. The pride of a man who, with his own hands and his own work, had managed to earn those fine linen sheets in which they both slept turning their backs on each other, and those delicacies that he ate with uneasiness under the eyes of that Trao wife of his.—But at least in his own house he wanted to call the tune himself. . . . Isabella should have everything he hadn't had, she should be a lady both in name and in fact. Bianca, as if she knew she didn't have long to live, didn't want to be separated from her daughter. But he was the master, Don Gesualdo. He was good, loving, in his own way; he didn't let her go without anything: doctors, drugs, exactly as if she had brought him a fat dowry" (pp. 235–36).

This rather complex passage is spoken by the usual popular narrator, who repeats Gesualdo's own remarks so faithfully as to let us hear his voice—a stylistic technique Verga had perfected in *Vita dei campi* and especially in *I Malavoglia*. In the text of the novel, the passage was prompted by Bianca's implied opposition to Gesualdo's decision to send Isabella to a faraway boarding school for the rich; but once it has begun rolling ahead, it quickly reaches much further than even the outer confines of a refutation—so much so that it turns into the lyrical synthesis of the entire narration.

Gesualdo offers us his own view of the reasons for his unhappiness and for his failures, yet he is completely unable to grasp them as such. Being unceasingly driven by economic motivations, he can only speak in the language of business. In his mind there is no conflict between monetary interests and human feelings. Even now, before his sick wife, he can state that he is a "good and loving" husband because he does not "let her go without any-thing . . . exactly as if she had brought him a fat dowry." In itself this assertion may sound monstrous, but it is instead perfectly logi-cal in a world such as Gesualdo's. He calls his marriage "a bad bargain"; and from his point of view it really was that. He did, in fact, marry Bianca for specific purposes: to rival with the aristocrats and the wealthy, and even to surpass and dominate them. Not only have these purposes remained largely unfulfilled, but they have forced him on a road of false values that is leading him to ruin, even in economic terms.

Characteristic is Gesualdo's attitude toward Isabella. He wants her to have everything, but all he does and all he gives serve exclu-sively to alienate her more. He cannot understand her profound involvement with Corrado La Gurna, in whom he sees but a greedy destitute who wants to get rich quickly. In Gesualdo's mind, his daughter and his property become identified; by protecting one, he feels he is protecting the other. His decision to have Isabella marry a nobleman from a great house is predicated on the conviction that, with money, his daughter will rise to heights he himself could not attain. But as a consequence, almost all his lands and a great deal of his money go to the Duke of Leyra—not just in the form of a dowry, but to indemnify him for a scandalous situation. Had Gesualdo allowed Isabella to marry Corrado La Gurna, everything would have proceeded regularly and without significant losses. This was not to pass, for, like the heroes of Greek tragedies, he carried within himself the logic of his own destruction and had to collaborate with his own merciless destiny. Ironically, but plausibly, the property he has valued so much will in its entirety go to the person (Isabella), who has been most sacrificed in its name, and who can least appreciate it. True, Gesualdo's failures are the product of his having unflinchingly obeyed his own economic drive. But he has also caused everyone else to fail. For everyone in the novel is a victim, and everyone is condemned to stand alone, in life as well as in death. The utter isolation born of greed, of ambition, and of the consequent inability to understand one another is the tragic theme of the novel. Verga explores it and develops it with extraordinary coherence.

Should we want to look at the novel from a purely sociological standpoint, we would note that, while Verga does manage to grasp the plight of the social climber, he also condemns him to bankruptcy, thereby proclaiming the validity of the continuity of the present order under the uninterrupted leadership of the existing aristocracy. Interestingly, Gesualdo's aristocratic daughter is not his daughter after all, and all of Gesualdo's wealth returns to the social class from which he had originally wrested it. A substantially different, though still sociological, view of our protagonist may suggest an essential affinity between Gesualdo and 'Ntoni Malavoglia, with the former being a far more advanced and, at least superficially, a far more successful version of the latter, in the sense that Gesualdo appears to fail also because he has reneged the solid values of his own social class. In both cases we may be led to conclude that Verga is thus permitting the conservative orientation of his bourgeois upbringing to function as a motivating force behind his work.

Ever since the beginning of this century the critics have been debating the relative merits of *I Malavoglia* and of *Mastro-don Gesualdo* in an effort to establish which one is the greater work. Benedetto Croce in 1903[6] and, still more resolutely, Luigi Russo in 1919,[7] opted for *I Malavoglia*, while Attilio Momigliano[8] declared

Mastro-don Gesualdo more varied and profound. From these pos-
tures sprang two opposite parties, which survived for half a century.
It goes without saying that they were indicative of the critics' literary training and their resulting personal preferences. Those who
exalted *Mastro-don Gesualdo* over and above all of Verga's other
works were generally rooted in the late Romantic tradition and were
impressed not only with the stature of the protagonist *per se*, but
also with sheer contents rather than with style; and they were often
unable to recognize that the novel did not constitute as powerful a
unified expressive and narrative whole as *I Malavoglia*. It is our
contention that the second novel of *I vinti* must be considered less
perfect than the first; yet it is undoubtedly a superb book in its own
right, and therefore it must be appreciated in all its richness and
complexity.

CHAPTER 6

Twilight

WITH *Mastro-don Gesualdo*, Verga concluded a decade of so intense a literary production as to establish himself as the greatest and the most innovative Italian writer of the second half of the nineteenth century. All his major works were published during that period. But at the end it was almost as if he had given everything he had. In fact, except for the solitary achievement of *Don Candeloro & C.*[i], after 1889 he lived a long twilight during which he first drifted toward inactivity, and then fell into it.

I   I ricordi del Capitano D'Arce *and* Don Candeloro & C.[i]

Most of the short stories collected in *I ricordi del Capitano D'Arce* (Captain D'Arce's Recollections), published in 1891, and at least one of those in *Don Candeloro & C.*[i], published in 1894, must be read as preparation for *La Duchessa di Leyra*, the third novel of the *I Vinti* series. Much of the first volume consists of a novelette in seven chapters devoted to the life and loves of a lady of the Neapolitan aristocracy, Ginevra—the rest being limited to the three already mentioned selections from *Drammi intimi*. Alternatively, Ginevra leaves her husband and selects her own lovers, drinking from the cup of passion until she finds death at its bottom. This time Verga does not make recourse to an invisible narrator, but tells his story in the words of a concrete and recognizable person, Captain D'Arce—who stands for Verga's other self. Thus he does not narrate in the words of his characters, but in his own. It is a method that may be reminiscent of the novels of his youth (Ginevra looks like a variation of Nata in *Tigre reale*). But now Verga has a much lighter hand, and views the selfishness and the hypocrisy of his men and women with the irony of experience.

As Romano Luperini has noted, even the passion of love, which stands at the very center of Ginevra's life, appears similar to an unending game which is being played according to the self-deceiving high society rules of simulation and dissimulation. In *Mastrodon Gesualdo*, the protagonist is always candid and straightforward; his conflicts with the local aristocracy are like the confrontations between what is real and vital and what is false and sterile. But now Verga seems to be intent on treating love like a comedy, and thereby on offering only its illusory and "non-authentic" side.[1] If anyone is in any way sincere, it is Ginevra, who is playing her game with full cognizance of what it is. But the most interesting character is her husband, a man who may appear tyrannical and violently jealous because he does not want to look ridiculous, but who is also the one to prove deeply human toward her. When she is gravely ill with consumption and all her lovers have abandoned her, he takes her back and affectionately watches over her during her last days. Verga, however, has not perceived the great possibilities implicit in such a character, and has, therefore, limited himself to a hurried sketch. It must be recognized, nevertheless, that his efforts to discover a refined and high-bourgeois language, and the emphasis he places on the female character and on the empty rhetoric of her life, are proof that *I ricordi del capitano D'Arce* are indeed a "study" for *La Duchessa di Leyra*, whose protagonist (Isabella) was conceived by Verga as desperately egotistical, vain, and unable to penetrate below the surface of life.[2]

Almost all of *Don Candeloro & C.*[i] consists of tales of poverty, many of which are of outstanding quality. It is true that in several of them certain situations resemble those already encountered in other narratives. "Papa Sisto," for instance, is reminiscent of "Il reverendo"; the new-rich Pecu-Pecu, in "L'opera del Divino Amore" (The Society of the Divine Love) of Don Gesualdo; the protagonist of "La vocazione di Suora Agnese" (Sister Agnes's Vocation) of *Storia di una capinera;* a paragraph or so of "Gl'Innamorati" (The Lovers) of "Cavalleria rusticana," etc. To those incidental similarities, however, we should not attribute any significance at all—for the stories are new and complex, and often written with consummate skill.

The first narratives, "Don Candeloro & C.[i]" and "Le marionette parlanti" (Talking Puppets), appear like two chapters of the same story. Don Candeloro makes his living with a puppet show. But soon he begins to lose his audience, for people are now demanding real actors. He decides to become a clown, but the public scorns him. Meanwhile, his daughter elopes with his apprentice, Martino—who does not want to marry her, however. With the passing of time Don Candeloro becomes more and more indulgent, until he finds himself eating at the tables of his daughter's lovers. It is another example of how poverty routs all moralistic qualms as well as all residue of personal pride. At the end we realize that the puppet show is the counterpart of the other show in which the characters are forced to play their roles at the orders of destiny. Like men in general, the transient actors on the stage of the world, the protagonists are the real puppets.

Similarly, in "Paggio Fernando" (Page Fernando) a stage director, with the pretext of casting Giuseppe Giacosa's *Una partita a scacchi* (A Chess Game), exploits a rich young man who falls in love with his daughter. The young man brings father and daughter large amounts of food, which he steals from his household. It is once more the case of the shrewd and the experienced blazenly exploiting the naïve, as was the case of Niní Rubiera in *Mastro-don Gesualdo*.

"La serata della diva" (The Star's Great Night) and "Il tramonto di Venere" (The Setting of Venus) are again like two parts of the same story. They portray two strikingly different periods in an actress's career. A star's hour of fame is brief, for life cannot be a continuous triumph, and success must be quickly followed by long misery. It is a late Romantic theme, which Verga presents from a variety of angles. In this particular case, the great actress gives herself so completely to the public that she does not even take notice of her numerous suitors. She cannot love anyone, for she belongs to everyone. This theme was to be taken up again by Luigi Pirandello, who gave it new depth and new implications in *Trovarsi* (To Find Oneself)—whose protagonist lives a thousand roles and assumes a thousand personalities, and as a result can never be herself, nor can she love anyone.

The other stories seem to be woven on a great number of different themes. An ambitious peasant puts his Machiavellian shrewdness to work and manages to become the father superior of a monastery, and thus do whatever he wants while ruling others with an iron hand ("Papa Sisto"). Two handsome priests come to preach in a convent, causing great turmoil among the nuns ("L'opera del Divino Amore"). A girl is engaged to a rich man, but as he discovers that her impoverished father has no money for her dowry, she convinces herself to enter a nunnery ("La vocazione di Suora Agnese"). A young man seduces the daughter of a rich merchant with all sorts of

inflamed promises, but as soon as he finds out that her father will
not give her a dowry, he "resigns himself" to letting the girl marry
someone else ("Gli innamorati"). The heroes of a revolution are soon
involved in destruction, pillaging, and raping ("Epopea spicciola"—Plain Epic). A histrionic Lenten preacher upsets a narrow-
mindedly religious woman so much that she gives premature birth
right in the church. She accuses herself of all kinds of sins, but is
unable to confess to a single infidelity even at the point of death. Yet
her husband must live the rest of his life in a town where he is
thought to be a cuckold ("Il peccato di Donna Santa"). The concluding piece, "Fra le scene della vita" (Behind the Curtains of
Life), consists of four short tales exemplifying the pretenses and the
hypocrisies underlying men's and women's personal relations.

   Don Candeloro & C.[i] is an extremely varied book, and yet it is
very well unified, at least in the sense that the stories develop a
similar theme: life is a comedy of errors in which everyone of us is an
actor. In the opening lines of "Fra le scene della vita" Verga writes:

How many times, in the so-called dramas of life, pretense mixes so
thoroughly with reality as to blend with it and to become tragic—with the
result that the man who is forced to perform a role can do so to perfection,
with total conviction, just like great actors. . . . How many bitter comedies,
and how many sad actors! (p. 377)

Verga is now seeing mankind as a conglomerate of actors performing
on the stage of life—with individual men and women either choos-
ing their roles or finding them ready-made. In the first two stories
the puppets are the people involved; in the others the characters
behave in an essentially like manner. Suor Agnese acts out her part
so well that she believes that by becoming a nun she is fulfilling the
call of God himself; the protagonist of "Papa Sisto" manages to
convince everyone (and himself) that what he pretends to be is his
real self; the preacher in "Il peccato di Donna Santa" uses the pulpit
as a stage and evokes Hell so vividly that people think they are
seeing it; and Donna Santa's poor husband becomes the victim of his
wife's self-incriminations to the point of acquiring a new identity for
the rest of his life. Whether the role everyone must play is justified
or not, is irrelevant. What counts is that it is here. We find it very
significant that the central theme of Verga's last book of short stories
will be predominant in all of Pirandello's fiction and theater—the

only major difference being that Pirandello will translate it into the analogous theme of the mask that everyone must wear and that constitutes everyone's true identity. Pirandello will make that theme extraordinarily vital by discovering inside it the very essence of man in society. For Verga, on the other hand, it remains purely emblematic of the utter insignificance of man himself.

Thus with *Don Candeloro & C.*[i] Verga seems first to be opening the gates of the future and then to walk well beyond the threshold. Even the style is maintained on a high plateau, through such original forms as free indirect speech, again rendered like the natural pattern of narrative communication. Because it anticipates the most fertile theme of another great writer, because of its richness and its unity, because the fabric of the narration is again woven on the texture of the characters' words and thoughts, and finally because of its smooth and original style, *Don Candeloro & C.*[i] must be rated as third in importance among Verga's collections of short stories—behind *Vita dei campi* and *Novelle rusticane*, and ahead of *Per le vie*. It was Verga's swan song, his brief triumph after *Mastro-don Gesualdo*. It is a book that the critics have not as yet fully appraised.

II La Duchessa di Leyra *(The Duchess of Leyra)*

In 1894, after residing in Milan for twenty years, Verga moved back to Catania, where he was to stay until his death. One of the main private events of his life during those years consisted in his falling in love with Giselda Fojanesi—a Florentine girl he had met in 1869 and who had become the wife of Catania's poet laureate, Mario Rapisardi. Verga had seen her again during one of his frequent visits to his native city, and soon the affair had flourished, lasting until December 1883, when Giselda's husband had suddenly learned about it and had sent her back to Florence. Following Rapisardi's discovery, Verga had expected to be challenged to a duel, but nothing of the kind had taken place. With Giselda alone and free in Florence one could have expected a near-normal relationship to develop between the two lovers. However, this would not occur, for Verga had never been able to encourage the maturation of any ties that could be translated into a permanent commitment.

It was also during the early 1880's that Verga met Dina Castellazzi de Sordevolo, then slightly more than twenty years old. This time the bond that developed between the two was to last the rest of his life. At first, owing to the fact that Dina was married, the affair was kept extremely secret. In 1891 Count Sordevolo died, and around 1893, after a brief interruption, the relationship began again. From then on Dina lived in the constant hope that Verga would marry her. It was possibly because of this hope that she accepted her lover's idiosyncracies—such as making sure that they were never seen together in public and having their occasional *rendezvous* only in faraway towns in Northern Italy, and only when Verga was free to travel. Verga wrote her over seven hundred letters (the last one dated December 28, 1921),[3] which constitute the main source of information on the last twenty years of his life. From them he emerges as extremely cautious and sometimes rather petty especially in his approach to financial matters.[4] But he assisted Dina by regularly sending her money, by trying to find publishers for her translations, and by giving her the rights for possible movie adaptations of his novels. Yet he always warded off her more or less veiled references to marriage.

In Catania Verga was not spared worries and afflictions. He had to act as a father to his brother's children and care for their land holdings. In 1896 he wrote to Dina: "I find myself burdened with all kinds of family trouble—I who have always managed to steer clear of it!" (Letter of June 12)—a remark which sheds light on some of the motives for his avoiding marriage with such determination. He also seemed to be harried by money problems and above all by the interminable litigations over the rights on the source material for Pietro Mascagni's *Cavalleria rusticana.*

In his letters Verga mentions his work in progress, *La Duchessa di Leyra,* rather often; once he even tells Dina that the king's visit to Catania presented a spectacle that very closely resembled the first chapter of *La Duchessa* (Letter of April 18, 1907). Many references to the new novel are also extant in Verga's letters to his translator, Edouard Rod. In two of them (one dated as early as November 30, 1898) he even discusses his plans for a French version of the novel.[5]

To become more familiar with the city where the action of *La Duchessa di Leyra* was to take place and to acquaint himself with the old court protocol, in 1895 Verga visited Palermo, which until 1860 had been the second capital of the Kingdom of the Two Sicilies. He then wrote a list of characters, specifying their moral and physical features, and establishing the relevant dates of the action—the same type of plan he had prepared before beginning *I Malavoglia.*

The Duchess of Leyra is Isabella Motta Trao, Mastro don Gesualdo's "daughter," whose illegitimate child is growing up in a convent. As her sexual mores are rather relaxed, she is constantly on the lookout for a new lover. Her penniless husband lives under the same roof only because she is rich and he must "come to terms with need." Around her there were to be many of her own aristocratic competitors, and a number of gentlemen. But the novel as such slowly faded away. When Verga died, in January 1922, his close friend, the writer Federico De Roberto, searched through his papers and found only a list of characters, some scanty notes, a general sketch, the first chapter, and the beginning of the second. In all those years Verga had not been able to write more. The reasons are in a letter of July 14, 1899, to his translator. After declaring that in his novels and short stories he had tried to put himself in the shoes of his characters, and after adding that this was what he was now attempting to do also in *La Duchessa di Leyra,* he observes that to speak the language of the higher social classes is extremely difficult—for at those levels people wear a common mask that forces them to express themselves through nuances and understatements, in a uniform medium which is nearly international in its tones and implications. It is, therefore, impossible to put oneself in their shoes and to speak their language. Then he concluded: "May God help me with this *Duchessa!*"[6] Significantly, he had been able to understand and give voice to the poor illiterate peasants of Sicily, but could not do so with the men and women of a social class much closer to his own. We may add that the fact that the *Duchessa* chapter published by De Roberto carries the mark of sarcasm in almost every paragraph seems to indicate that Verga did not approve of a society rooted in false pretenses, corrupt and parasitical. Yet he was unable to expose it and condemn it.

III Dal tuo al mio (*What's Yours Is Mine*)

Written and performed as a play in 1903, *Dal tuo al mio* was later published as a novel, first in the journal *Nuova Antologia* (1905) and then in book form by Treves in 1906.[7] The transition was chiefly achieved by filling in the characters' appearances and gestures—as well as whatever was originally relegated to the stage directions— and by leaving the dialogue untouched. In the process Verga occasionally introduced a few tense and vibrant passages that were caught on the lips of an invisible spectator turned narrator. Generally, however, the characters' features—the color of their faces, the emotional and nonemotional grimaces—are presented from the outside. They are not created by their words, by the instinctive coincidence between their inner and outer human substance. In its final form *Dal tuo al mio* is neither a play nor a novel.

On the occasion of the engagement of his daughter Nina to Don Nunzio Rametta's son, Baron Navarra is having a reception. But, instead of the fiancé, the father shows up—for he has discovered that Navarra's sulfur mine is beset by debt and, consequently, he does not want a daughter-in-law whose family is almost bankrupt. Nina, who is in love with her cousin but has agreed to marry someone else only to help her father financially, is aware that the new development will cause her to remain an old maid, as she herself suggests in a moving passage that must be considered the high point in the entire work. Her sister Lisa, however, wants to take care of her own future and—unmindful of the aristocratic family name—entices her father's handsome foreman, Luciano. The baron must borrow money from Rametta to put the mine back into production, and thus he must agree to give Rametta all the profits for a number of years. Luciano, who now works for Rametta, manages to convince his co-workers to strike for higher wages. Rametta does not give in, and the workers threaten to set fire to the mine. Now Luciano, whose wife Lisa will eventually become half owner of the mine, allies himself with Rametta in order to protect the property. To stifle the workers' uprising, Rametta decides to call in the army.

The characters are rather sketchy. Luciano's about-face is too abrupt, Rametta thinks and acts like a crudely undeveloped Mastro-don Gesualdo, while Baron Navarra, in spite of all his class vanity, stands out as a man of integrity. These shortcomings of the novel are rooted in an excessive preoccupation with the social message Verga wants to convey through Luciano. On the surface people may engage in a class struggle, but actually it is by self-interest that all their actions are motivated. Apparently, Verga has reached the point when he perceives only the most squalid of human realities, and completely ignores any form of idealism. His inability to understand the march of the times and his congenital reactionism have finally come to the fore to overpower his creative energies.

IV   *The Theater*

Ever since his early youth Verga dreamed of becoming a great playwright. He devoted himself to this activity on and off during the entire span of his productive years, revealing the same expressive and stylistic trajectory as through his novels and short stories. He was still living in Catania when he unsuccessfully submitted *I nuovi Tartufi* (The New Tartuffes), a play now lost, to a national competition.[8] After moving to Florence, in 1869 he wrote *Rose Caduche* (Fading Roses), which, as we have seen, was highly praised by the then renowned critic Francesco Dall'Ongaro,[9] but never reached the stage. It was published posthumously in the June 1928 issue of *Maschere*.

Rose caduche must be placed on approximately the same level as Verga's early novels. Its plot is very similar to the story of *Una peccatrice;* in some respects it even foreshadows the most pronouncedly sentimental themes of *Tigre reale*. The protagonist, Irma Scotti, is frantically clinging to an illusion of eternal love, even after her lover has tired of her. Incapable of following "Una peccatrice" in suicide, she remains desperately alone. The play is long, overflowing with emphatic speeches and repetitions. It thoroughly mirrors the young writer, still unable to perceive the explosive vitality that can lie within simple words.

When he yielded again to the temptation of writing for the stage, Verga had attained the heights of maturity. In a few days of the late summer 1883 he rewrote his short story "Cavalleria rusticana" as a one-act tragedy. We do not know what persuaded him to undertake this work, although it is conceivable that he was influenced by his friendship with Giuseppe Giacosa, the leading playwright of the time, and with Arrigo Boito, a man of the theater and a composer of considerable genius. It is certain, however, that with *Cavalleria rusticana* Verga applied to the theater the same principles of objectivity as those he had adopted for his narrative works, and therefore he produced a totally unusual work. He submitted the manuscript to a "Readers' Committee," consisting of Boito, Treves, Luigi Gualdo, and Eugenio Torelli-Viollier (the editor of *Corriere della sera*). Torelli-Viollier was the only one to express a favorable opinion—the others pronouncing the play much too realistic and not suitable for staging. Then Verga gave the manuscript to Giacosa, who read it with enthusiasm and had the play performed in Turin on January 14, 1884, starring three of the greatest actors Italy could boast at the time—Eleanora Duse, Cesare Rossi, and Tebaldo Checchi. It was the greatest dramatic success that had been seen in many a year, and the only great success Verga enjoyed during his life.

Superficially, the drama repeats the plot of the short story as well

as its central theme. But in reality it complicates them in such a way
as to elicit substantial changes. In the story Turiddu tries to seduce
Santa for the purpose of making Lola jealous; he is not interested in
Santa, but in Lola, whom he wants back for himself—especially now
that she is married to someone else. The problem arises when Santa
herself gets deeply involved and causes his destruction. In the play
Santa becomes one of the main determinants of the action. She is
pregnant by Turiddu and wants him for herself. Lola is the one to be
jealous and to seduce Turiddu, because her ego cannot tolerate his
being someone else's lover. And Turiddu's mother is no longer a
silent presence in the background, but is vocally resentful of Santa,
in whom she unconsciously sees a competitor for her son's affection.

So great is the importance Santa acquires in the play that she
almost turns into the real protagonist. She is even at the center of
Turiddu's last words. He in fact says that, although guilty, he will do
everything to kill Alfio because he has an obligation toward
Santa—while in the short story Turiddu declares himself motivated
by his desire not to hurt his mother. This very significant change
represents, as Bergin puts it, a "rather puzzling" reversion.[10] Indeed, the original clash between Turiddu's feelings toward his
mother and those of Alfio—who with his third stab implied that his
own sufferings were of the same nature ("And that's three! That's for
making me a cuckold in my own house. Now your mother will let
the chickens alone"), is lost.[11] Verga further modifies his original
conception of the characters by making Santa very poor and Turiddu
rich—the opposite of how they fared in the story. This was probably
intended to suggest that Turiddu was particularly insensitive and
egotistical, and that consequently Santa deserves understanding and
indulgence for seeking her revenge. Yet Turiddu, in the crowded
scene in which he offers wine to the villagers, appears like the
victim soon to be sacrificed for the sins of everyone else. It seems
clear that Verga tried to assuage the bourgeois tastes of his spectators by making the plot more readily understandable and more
acceptable.

On still closer scrutiny we will find that artistically the play is
definitely inferior to the short story. It is less condensed, less
straightforward, and written in a language which is somewhat
amorphous and colorless. It is the language of the bourgeois spectators rather than the characters'. Verga himself believed the story
superior to the play.[12] However, *Cavalleria rusticana* remains a

work of fundamental importance in the history of modern Italian theater. It marked the end of the staging of the ineffectual and nebulous plots of medieval extraction, and the beginning of the new realistic drama. After *Cavalleria,* even Giacosa committed himself to writing about contemporary society and contemporary problems.

A welcomed example of tragic intensity, Verga's play continued to be represented with great success. In 1889 Giovanni Targioni-Tozzetti and Giovanni Menasci, upon request by a penniless and obscure young composer, Pietro Mascagni, rewrote it in the form of an opera libretto. The new musical drama was submitted by Mascagni to the famous 1890 Sonzogno competition, and it placed first. To make its performance possible, the composer had to secure the permission of Giovanni Verga, who consented without establishing a rate of compensation. The unprecedented enthusiasm with which the opera was received all over the world was to turn into the cause for a long and bitter litigation between Verga on one side and Edoardo Sonzogno and Pietro Mascagni on the other. The first phase of the litigation ended in 1893, when in final settlement Verga was awarded a one-time-only sum of 143,000 lire (more than $600,000 in today's money). But a few years later Verga brought suit again on grounds that his 1893 consent had been "fraudulently extorted." During a period of many years he incurred heavy legal costs, of which he was able to recover less than half. He doggedly continued, until, with Italy's entrance into World War I in 1915, the litigation began to fade away.[13]

In 1902, in an effort to replace Mascagni's work with a new and equally popular *Cavalleria* which would give him an established percentage of the receipts, Verga allowed a composer, Domenico Monleone, to set to music another libretto derived from the same original one-act play. Thus for a while the theaters of Europe staged two different *Cavalleria rusticanas.* But as Monleone's opera attained the first success in Italy, Sonzogno quickly went to court alleging unlawful imitation, illegal and unfair competition, and finally illicit authorization by Verga. That was the end of the other *Cavalleria.*

Meanwhile, the success of his own drama had encouraged Verga to continue writing plays by adapting some of his better-known short stories, and by extracting from them and making explicit as much as possible of what had originally been suggested between the lines. In 1885 he rewrote "Il canarino del N. 15," (a story from *Per le vie*) as a two-act play by the title of *In portineria* (The Porter's Lodging). To meet stage requirements, some episodes were added and an effort was made to give fuller development to some of the characters. The fundamentally important economic theme, which in the story had remained in the background, was so emphasized as to have it turn into one of the main movers of the action. But again the characters' words do not create an environment nor do they evoke an inner tension. *In portineria* was premiered in Milan on May 16, 1885, and it was a failure.

In January 1896, when Verga was in the midst of his second litigation over Mascagni's *Cavalleria rusticana*, *La lupa* (The She-wolf) was premiered in Turin with moderate success. The brief, suggestive, and extraordinarily intense short story had been transposed into a two-act tragedy. If there is one work that proves how unsuited Verga was for the theater, this is "La lupa." Most of the events are internal and presented in such a way that the reader perceives them by implication and by association. The mere discussion of them on stage causes them to lose their poignancy and even their substance. Again to make his story visibly believable, Verga is forced to interpolate several entire scenes, and to dilute others. Nanni, for instance, who in the story was the victim of the inescapability of the flesh, is transformed into a man who is especially interested in property. This new element makes the plot deviate toward an unexpected tangent. It does not totally replace the main theme, but it most assuredly weakens it. Verga himself tells us that such a thematic dichotomy is intentional. When he presents his cast of characters (for the first time he indulges in detailed introductions), he defines Nanni as "a handsome young man, tender with women, but still more so with his own interests." Another novelty of importance occurs in the first act. Mara refuses to marry Nanni because she knows of her mother's affair with him. This, of course, is not in the story, and undoubtedly it affects the credibility of the situation—even if it is intended to prove unequivocally how thoroughly Mara is dominated by her mother.

In the story there is a complete correspondence between the passion burning inside the protagonist's flesh and its external counterpart—the searing landscape. No one can forget the afternoon hour when the She-wolf awakens Nanni. In the drama this correspondence is lost. Nor is such loss compensated for by the stage directions at the beginning of the acts—two veritably poetic passages, in spite of their being purely tangential to the action.

It must be finally noted that in *La lupa* Verga has utilized some folklore elements, such as the prolonged rustic dances absorbed into the first act. This device probably indicates that the new drama was written as a result of the success of Mascagni's opera, and with an eye to its possible adaptation as a libretto. Indeed, two or three years before its performance Verga discussed a libretto version with Federico De Roberto and approached Giacomo Puccini about setting it to music. The composer decided to travel to Sicily for the purpose of picking up a few local musical themes to be incorporated in the opera. He even wrote some fragments, but kept declaring himself dissatisfied with the text. He finally said that before committing himself to the opera, he wanted to see how the original drama would come off on the stage, and gave up the project. Puccini did not feel at home with elemental peasant dramas; by abandoning *La lupa*, he actually followed the dictates of his own artistic temperament. The musical fragments he had already composed ended up in his next opera, *La Bohème*.[14]

La caccia al lupo (The Wolf Hunt) is the 1901 adaptation of a story by the same title, originally published in 1897. With unfailing shrewdness a cuckolded shepherd traps his wife with her lover in his own house, and then prepares his vengeance. Both the short story and the play are based on a popular analogy, and both march toward their conclusion without deviations. In the play the personalities of the lovers are developed more fully. Characteristically, as soon as they find themselves trapped, they have no tender feelings left in them, and each one is preoccupied with his, or her, own safety.

During the same period Verga wrote another one-act sketch. *La caccia alla volpe* (The Fox Hunt). This time the action takes place in the higher echelon of society. A marchioness resents that her lover almost encourages her to yield to other would-be seducers. She enjoys being courted, but at the same time she wants to belong to a possessive man. The short play can be defined as no more than a society game.

La caccia al lupo and *La caccia alla volpe* were written to be performed together and with the intent of exploring two similar situations in two totally different social milieux. Again Verga is more successful with the first, which once again portrays the elemental world of the Sicilian peasants. He still finds it very difficult to present the empty egotism of high society. At this point, as we approach the end of his history, we must recognize that Verga's inability to penetrate—and therefore to portray convincingly—the vain pretenses and the congenital falsehoods of a decadent and parasitical high bourgeoisie and aristocracy, is the demonstration of his profound coherence.

In his last fifteen years Verga produced only a fairly insignificant short story, "Una capanna e il tuo cuore" (In a Hut with Your Heart)—a sardonic description of a few hours in the life of poor vaudeville actors and an account, as the writer himself told De Roberto, "of where the dreams of life lead to," as well as of how his own "literary aspirations" were ending.[15] It was written in 1919 and published posthumously in February 1922.

In Catania Verga chose to be alone and isolated, and always tried to protect his solitude. He had some financial worries, but they appeared to decrease with time. In September 1920, in Catania's Teatro Massimo, Italy officially celebrated the eightieth birthday of the great writer, with Pirandello as the official speaker. But it was too little and too late. Verga disdainfully refused to attend. A month later, Prime Minister Giovanni Giolitti, informed him that he had been appointed a Senator of the Kingdom (a tradition that had initiated with Alessandro Manzoni in 1860). Verga, however, did not show much appreciation. On the night of January 24, 1922, he had just stopped reading *Natio borgo selvaggio* (My Barbarous Native Town) by the Florentine Ferdinando Paolieri, when he suffered an attack of cerebral hemorrhage. He never regained his senses, and in the early morning of January 27, as De Roberto puts it, "immortality began."[16]

Notes and References

Chapter One

1. Cf. "Il maestro di G. Verga," and other chapters in Federico De Roberto, *Casa Verga*, a cura di C. Musumarra (Firenze, 1964).
2. Giulio Cattaneo, *Giovanni Verga* (Torino, 1963), p. 27.
3. Cf. *Studi verghiani*, I (edizioni del Sud, 1929).
4. Cf. G. Verga, *I carbonari della montagna, Sulle lagune*, Saggio introduttivo di Carlo Annoni (Milano, 1975).
5. On *Sulle lagune*, in addition to the already-mentioned essay by Annoni, see a study by Gian Paolo Biasin, "Il romanzo *Sulle lagune* del giovane Verga," *La rassegna della letteratura italiana*, 74, 2–3 (1970), pp. 394–416.
6. All the quotes from *Una peccatrice*, as well as from the following three novels, are drawn from G. Verga, *Una peccatrice, Storia di una capinera, Eva, Tigre reale* (BMM, Milano, 1943). A note on p. 8 regarding *Una peccatrice* reads as follows: "This novel was publicly repudiated in 1892 by its author on the occasion of its then being reissued in Catania. It is now . . . republished on the basis of its documentary significance [in its author's career]."
7. Luigi Russo, *Giovanni Verga* (Bari, 1947), p. 45.
8. Carmelo Musumarra, *Il Verga minore* (Pisa, 1965), pp. 50, 56–58.
9. Gaetano Ragonese, *Interpretazioni verghiane* (Palermo, 1965), pp. 25–26.
10. Aurelio Navarria, *Lettura di poesia nell'opera di Giovanni Verga* (Messina-Firenze, 1962), p. 19.
11. Federico De Roberto, pp. 135–142.
12. Luigi Russo, p. 53.
13. On *Scapigliatura*, cf. Pietro Nardi, *La scapigliatura* (Bologna, 1924); Angelo Romanò, *Il secondo romanticismo lombardo* (Milano, 1958); and especially Gaetano Mariani, *Storia della scapigliatura* (Caltanisetta-Roma, 1967). In Mariani's monumental work the influence of the *scapigliati* on Verga is discussed in the two concluding chapters.
14. Cf. Attilio Momigliano, *Impressioni di un lettore contemporaneo* (Milano, 1928), chapter on *Eva*.

15. Cf. G. Verga, *Lettere a Dina*, a cura di Gino Raya (Roma, 1962; new enlarged edition, retitled *Lettere d'amore*, 1971), pp. VII–VIII, and letters of August 29, September 24, and October 14, 1920.

16. Giulio Marzot, *Preverismo, Verga e la generazione verghiana* (Bologna, 1965), p. 38.

17. In the issue of January 16, 1874. In a letter to Capuana dated April 5, 1873 (cf. G. Verga, *Lettere a Luigi Capuana*, Firenze, 1975, pp. 37–38), Verga himself stated that he feared the novel would be criticized because it was too "loose" and because it called "a spade a spade." However, the context of the letter indicated pride, rather than apprehension.

18. Cf. Ferdinando Martini's article *"Eva,"* in *Fra un sigaro e l'altro* (Milano, 1876).

19. All the *Eros* quotations are from G. Verga, *Eros, Il marito di Elena* (Milano, 1946).

20. Benedetto Croce, *La letteratura della Nuova Italia* (Bari, reprinted many times), vol. III, p. 10.

21. Luigi Russo, p. 65.

22. Giacomo De Benedetti, *Saggi critici*, Terza serie (Milano, 1961), p. 277, and *Verga e il naturalismo* (Milano, 1976), p. 237.

23. Carmelo Musumarra, pp. 109, 126.

24. Aurelio Navarria, p. 40. As in other cases, my brief critical survey is limited to those critics whose opinions have been influential in Verga scholarship.

25. Cf. Riccardo Scrivano, "Il Verga tra scapigliatura e verismo," *Belfagor*, XXI (1965), pp. 653–63; especially, pp. 660–61.

26. Roberto Bigazzi, *I colori del vero* (Pisa, 1969), pp. 383–92.

27. Gian Paolo Marchi, *Concordanze verghiane* (Verona, 1970), pp. 33–36.

28. The quotations from "Nedda," as well as from all the other short stories, are derived from the standard edition, G. Verga, *Tutte le novelle* (Milano, 1940, reprinted many times), 2 vols. The first volume has *Novelle* (which includes "Nedda"), *Vita dei campi, Novelle rusticane,* and *Per le vie;* the second volume, *Vagabondaggio, I ricordi del Capitano D'Arce, Don Candeloro e C.ⁱ, Dal tuo al mio,* and the stories Verga left scattered in magazines.

29. *Nuova Antologia*, Roma, luglio, 1874, p. 813.

30. Luigi Capuana, *Studi sulla letteratura italiana contemporanea* (Catania, 1882), p. 117.

31. Benedetto Croce, p. 15.

32. Thomas G. Bergin, *Giovanni Verga* (New Haven, 1931; reissued in 1969 by the Greenwood Press, Wesport, Conn.), pp. 38–41. All page references are made to the first printing.

33. Cf. Gaetano Ragonese, p. 40; Carmelo Musumarra, pp. 143–57; and especially my own study, "La 'Nedda' del Verga," *Belfagor*, XV (1960), reprinted in my *Il Verga maggiore* (Firenze, 1968, 1970, 1973), pp. 1–25.

34. Cf. G. Verga, *Vita dei campi: Novelle illustrate da Arnaldo Ferraguti* (Milano, 1897). On the text of this volume, cf. my essay, "Il testo di *Vita dei campi* e le correzioni verghiane, "*Belfagor*, XII (1957), reprinted in my *Il Verga maggiore*, pp. 47–78.

35. Cf. Verga's letters to Emilio Treves, edit. by Lina e Vito Perroni in "Storia de *I Malavoglia*," *Nuova Antologia*, 16 marzo and 1 aprile, 1940.

36. Gaetano Mariani, pp. 659–60.

37. Olga Ragusa, *Verga's Milanese Stories* (New York, 1964), p. 27.

Chapter Two

1. *Corriere della sera*, 9–10, settembre 1877. Quoted in Aurelio Navarria, p. 70.

2. G. Verga, *Lettere a Luigi Capuana*, p. 114.

3. Cf. Riccardo Artuffo, "Interviste siciliane. Giovanni Verga," *La Tribuna*, Roma, 2 febbraio 1911. Also Benedetto Croce reported the story (cf. *La critica*, 20 gennaio 1916).

4. Of the works of Francesco De Sanctis there are many excellent editions. The first of the two quotations can be found in the "Introduzione" to *Saggio critico sul Petrarca*, and the second at the end of "Zola e l'Assommoir," *Saggi critici*, III. This latter essay is the stenographic text of a lecture delivered in 1879.

5. Claude Bernard's book is the well-known *Introduction à la medicine expérimentelle*, published in 1865, and Emile Zola's declaration may be found at the beginning of his *Roman expérimental*. Although written many years later, *Le roman expérimental* presents substantially the same theories as those Zola had first developed in the 1868 preface to *Thérèse Raquin* (cf. John C. Lapp, *Zola before the "Rougon-Macquart*," Toronto, 1964, p. 89).

6. Cf. G. Verga, "Lettere inedite, raccolte e annotate da Maria Borgese," *Occidente*, 20 maggio, 1935.

7. Ugo Ojetti, *Alla scoperta dei letterati*, a cura di Pietro Pancrazi (Firenze, 1946; 1st edition, Milano, 1895), pp. 117–18.

8. Many studies of the psychology of the masses, or, as they called it, of demopsychology, were then being undertaken. They were based on a tremendous amount of documentary material gathered in the provinces with the intent of preserving, and emphasizing the significance of, popular traditions. The greatest scholar in the field was the Sicilian Giuseppe Pitré, whose 1872 *Storia della poesia popolare* exerted considerable influence on the literature of the time. Pitré collected documents of popular traditions and folklore to fill twenty-five volumes. Girolamo Ragusa-Moleti, a novelist

who was also a scholar, exploited Sicilian folklore themes for his tales. He is considered of importance in the development of the local aspects of *verismo* (cf. Luigi Russo, *I narratori*, Milano-Messina, 1951, p. 145). On *verismo* there exists a fairly large bibliography, but very few are the works combining good information with reliable criticism. We shall mention only the following: Luigi Russo, Introduction to *I narratori*; Giulio Marzot, *Battaglie veristiche dell'Ottocento* (Milano-Messina, 1941); Mario Marcazzan, "Dal romanticismo al decadentismo," *Letteratura italiana. Le correnti* (Milano, 1956), pp. 663–896; and Roberto Bigazzi, *I colori del vero, op. cit.*

9. Cf. Luigi Capuana's lecture, "La Sicilia nei canti popolari e nella novellistica contemporanea," published in the miscellaneous volume, *L'Isola del sole* (Catania, 1898). On Capuana as a novelist, a critic, and the theoretician of *verismo*, cf. Carlo A. Madrignani, *Capuana e il naturalismo* (Bari, 1970), and Gaetano Trombatore, "La critica di Luigi Capuana e la poetica del verismo," in *Riflessi letterari de Risorgimento in Sicilia e altri studi secondo Ottocento* (Palermo, 1970).

10. Ugo Ojetti, p. 116.

11. Luigi Russo, p. 409.

12. Leo Spitzer, "L'originalità della narrazione ne *I Malavoglia*," *Belfagor*, XI (1956), pp. 37–53; and my article, "Aspetti della prosa di *Vita dei campi*," Italica, XXXIV (1957), now in my *Il Verga maggiore*, pp. 27–46. On Verga's narrative language, see also Vitilio Masiello, "La lingua del Verga tra mimesi dialettale e realismo critico," in Alberto Asor Rosa, *Il caso Verga* (Palermo, 1974), pp. 89–117.

13. G. Verga, *Lettere al suo traduttore*, a cura di Fredi Chiappelli (Firenze, 1954), pp. 130–31.

14. Cf. The closing lines of De Sanctis's "Zola e l'*Assommoir*."

15. G. Verga, *Lettere al suo traduttore*, p. 245.

16. This fact was revealed for the first time by Lina and Vito Perroni in their prefatory remarks to "Storia de *I Malavoglia*."

17. Luigi Russo, p. 106.

18. Romano Luperini, *Verga e le strutture narrative del realismo* (Padova, 1976), pp. 110–11. This volume consists of an extended, and significant, essay on "Rosso Malpelo." Luperini has discovered that an early version of the short story was published in the Roman daily *Il Fanfulla* in August 1878 (cf. pp. 1–2). It is an important find, for it proves that Verga had already attained a high degree of artistic maturity while he was planning the cycle of *I vinti* and slowly turning his *Padron 'Ntoni* into *I Malavoglia*. It must be remembered, on the other hand, that "Rosso Malpelo" was not the first of the *Vita dei campi* stories to be written. "Fantasticheria," in fact, although published only in 1879, was most probably already completed by January 1878 (cf. Vito Perroni, "Sulla genesi de *I Malavoglia*," *Le ragioni critiche*, 6 (1972), p. 513, n. 37).

19. The definitive text of "Pentolaccia" appeared in the 1897 edition of

Vita dei campi: Novelle illustrate da Arnaldo Ferraguti, and was later reprinted in *Tutte le novelle*, vol. I. The 1880 text was stylistically different. Cf. my *Il Verga maggiore*, pp. 58 ff.

Chapter Three

1. This letter, dated April 21, 1878, was first published in *Giornale dell'Isola*, 22 gennaio 1922, and later reproduced in Giulio Cattaneo, pp. 161–62.
2. G. Verga, *Lettere al suo traduttore*, pp. 130–31.
3. G. Verga, *Lettere a Luigi Capuana*, p. 114.
4. Cf. Lina e Vito Perroni, "Storia de *I Malavoglia*," p. 111.
5. This outline was printed in G. Verga, *I Malavoglia* (Milano, "Oscar" Mondadori, 1970), pp. 17–20.
6. Cf. Lina e Vito Perroni, "Storia de *I Malavoglia*," p. 124.
7. On this subject cf. my essay, "I carro e il mare amaro," *Il Verga maggiore*, pp. 82–96.
8. Thomas G. Bergin, p. 110.
9. Giacomo Devoto, *Nuovi studi di stilistica* (Firenze, 1961), pp. 202–14, but especially p. 214.
10. Edoardo Scarfoglio, *Il libro di don Chisciotte* [1885] (Milano, 1925), p. 99.
11. *Luigi Capuana*, in *Il Fanfulla della domenica*, maggio 1881.
12. Cf. closing lines of Francesco De Sanctis's essay, "Zola e l'*Assommoir.*"
13. Leopoldo Franchetti and Sidney Sonnino, *La Sicilia 1876* (Firenze, 1876; reprinted 1925).
14. Francesco Torraca, "*I Malavoglia*," *Saggi e rassegne* (Livorno, 1885).
15. G. Verga, *Lettere a Luigi Capuana*, p. 168.
16. Cf. G. Verga, "Lettere inedite a Carlo Del Balzo," a cura di Salvatore Pescatori, *La ruota*, settembre 1940.
17. G. Verga, *Lettere al suo traduttore*, p. 39.
18. Benedetto Croce, p. 32. Croce's essay was first published in *La critica*, 1903.
19. Luigi Russo, pp. 157–225, especially 219–25.
20. Cf. Leo Spitzer, Giacomo Devoto, and my own "Aspetti della prosa di *Vita dei campi*," *Il Verga maggiore*, pp. 22–46.
21. Romano Luperini, *Pessimismo e verismo in Giovanni Verga* (Padova, 1969), pp. 75–104.

Chapter Four

1. Cf. Lina e Vito Perroni, "Storia de *I Malavoglia*," *Nuova Antologia*, April 1, 1940, p. 239, n. 1.
2. G. Verga, *Lettere a Luigi Capuana*, p. 189.

3. All the quotes from *Il marito di Elena* are from *Eros, Il marito di Elena*.

4. G. Verga, *Lettere al suo traduttore*, p. 52.

5. G. Verga, *Tutte le novelle*, vol. I, p. 346.

6. On this subject cf. Verga's own statement in *Lettere a Dina* (now *Lettere d'amore*), letter dated June 12, 1896.

7. G. Verga, *Lettere a Luigi Capuana*, p. 191. With his usual critical acumen, Verga remained convinced that *Il marito di Elena* had not turned out to be as good a novel as he had hoped (cf. *Lettere al suo traduttore*, pp. 50–51).

8. Thomas G. Bergin, p. 67.

9. Luigi Russo, p. 266.

10. G. Verga, *Lettere a Luigi Capuana*, p. 49.

11. For a well-balanced opinion on *Il marito di Elena*, cf. Roberto Bigazzi, pp. 439–42.

12. Fredi Chiappelli, "Una lettura verghiana," *Lettere italiane*, XII (1960), p. 24.

13. For a detailed analysis of the entire story, cf. my essay, " 'Pane nero'," *Il Verga maggiore*, pp. 115–53.

14. For an analysis of "Libertà," cf. my "A note to Verga's 'Freedom,' " *Italian Quarterly*, 60–61 (1972), pp. 79–89.

15. Some years ago, Olga Ragusa, in her *Verga's Milanese Tales*, made a sustained effort to demonstrate that these short stories should be placed on the same artistic level as their author's "Sicilian" tales. While respecting Ms. Ragusa's opinions, we find them somewhat unconvincing.

16. Giulio Marzot, p. 87.

17. As already implied (cf. note 28 to Chapter I), all quotes from short stories beginning with, and following, the *Vagabondaggio* series are derived from G. Verga, *Tutte le novelle*, vol. II.

18. Luigi Russo, 292–93.

Chapter Five

1. On the question of the two versions of the novel, cf. Vittorio Lugli, "I due *Mastro-don Gesualdo*," *Dante e Balzac* (Napoli, 1952), pp. 243–49 (this essay first appeared in *Rivista d'Italia*, marzo 1925); Salvatore Lo Nigro, "Le due redazioni del *Mastro don-Gesualdo*." *Lettere italiane*, II (1949), pp. 5–28; Leone Piccioni, *Lettura leopardiana e altri saggi* (Firenze, 1952), pp. 254–68; my own "L'elaborazione della fine del *Mastro-don Gesualdo*," *Il Verga maggiore*, pp. 155–87; Francesco Nicolosi, *Questioni verghiane* (Roma, 1969), pp. 78–185; and Gian Paolo Marchi, *Concordanze verghiane*, pp. 118–26.

2. All quotations from *Mastro-don Gesualdo* are from the Milano, Mondadori, 1940 edition.

3. G. Verga, *Lettere al suo traduttore*, p. 139.

4. Giuseppe Petronio, *Dall'illuminismo al verismo* (Palermo, 1962), p. 243.

5. For a detailed analysis of this chapter, cf. my own "L'elaborazione della fine del *Mastro-don Gesualdo*."

6. Benedetto Croce, p. 32.

7. Luigi Russo, p. 364.

8. Cf. Attilio Momigliano, *Dante, Manzoni, Verga* (Messina-Firenze, 1944; reprinted 1955); but cf. especially the appendix, which reproduces the author's entry on "Verga, Giovanni," in *Enciclopedia italiana*, vol. XXXV.

Chapter Six

1. Cf. Romano Luperini, *L'orgoglio e la disperata rassegnazione* (Roma, 1974), p. 90.

2. Cf. Verga's sketches for the novel in Federico De Roberto, pp. 220, 224, 225.

3. Cf. G. Verga, *Lettere a Dina* (now *Lettere d'amore*).

4. Cf. my own review of *Lettere a Dina*, *Il ponte*, 1963, pp. 126–29.

5. Cf. G. Verga, *Lettere a Dina* (now *Lettere d'amore*), and *Lettere al suo traduttore*. In both cases the references to *La Duchessa di Leyra* are easily ascertainable by consulting the indexes.

6. Cf. G. Verga, *Lettere al suo traduttore*, pp. 130–31.

7. Verga never published the original stage version of *Dal tuo al mio*. It appeared for the first time in G. Verga, *Teatro* (Milano, 1952).

8. Federico De Roberto, p. 190.

9. Regarding the date of Verga's composition of *Rose caduche*, cf. Anna Barsotti, *Verga drammaturgo* (Firenze, 1974), pp. 10–12.

10. Thomas G. Bergin, p. 97.

11. Luigi Russo, p. 286.

12. Federico De Roberto, p. 189.

13. A somewhat biased account of Verga's lengthy litigations is in Alfred Alexander, *Giovanni Verga* (London, 1972), pp. 165–97.

14. Cf. Giulio Cattaneo, pp. 273–78. *La lupa* was finally set to music shortly before the outbreak of World War I by Pierantonio Tasca, but it was premiered only in 1933 in the Sicilian town of Noto, the composer's birthplace. To our knowledge, it has never been performed since then.

15. Gino Raya, *Bibliografia verghiana* (Roma, 1972), p. 252.

15. Federico De Roberto, p. 263.

Selected Bibliography

PRIMARY SOURCES

The following is a list of Verga's works in the most reliable editions available. Each of them has been reprinted several times. For the original publications, see the *Chronology* at the beginning of this volume.

I carbonari della montagna. Sulle lagune. Saggio introduttivo di Carlo Annoni. Milano: Vita e Pensiero, 1975.

Una peccatrice e altri racconti. Milano: Mondadori, 1943 (*Una peccatrice, Storia di una capinera, Eva, Tigre reale*).

Eros. Il marito di Elena. Milano: Mondadori, 1946.

Tutte le novelle, vol. I. Milano: Mondadori, 1940 (*Novelle* [originally: *Primavera ed altri racconti*], *Vita dei campi, Novelle rusticane, Per le vie*).

Tutte le novelle, vol. II. Milano: Mondadori, 1942 (*Vagabondaggio, I ricordi del Capitano D'Arce, Don Candeloro e C.¹, Dal tuo al mio,* "Appendice").

I Malavoglia. Milano: Mondadori, 1939.

Mastro-don Gesualdo. Milano: Mondadori, 1940.

Teatro. Milano: Mondadori, 1952 (*Cavalleria rusticana, In portineria, La lupa, La caccia al lupo, La caccia alla volpe, Rose caduche, Dal tuo al mio, Dopo*).

Translations

The translations available (not all of them fully reliable) are very few:

The House by the Medlar Tree (I Malavoglia). Translated by Raymond Rosenthal. New York: New American Library, Signet Classics, 1964.

The She-Wolf and Other Stories. Translated by Giovanni Cecchetti. University of California Press, Berkeley–Los Angeles–London: 1973. Contains the best of *Vita dei campi* and of *Novelle rusticane*, in addition to a selection of short stories from other volumes.

163

Mastro-don Gesualdo. Translated by D. H. Lawrence. New York: Grove Press, 1955, reissued by the Greenwood Press, Westport, Conn., 1976.
Little Novels of Sicily (Novelle rusticane). Translated by D. H. Lawrence. London: Penguin Modern Classics, 1973.
Cavalleria Rusticana and Other Stories. Translated by D. H. Lawrence. Westport, Conn.: Greenwood Press, 1975.
Cavalleria Rusticana, Nine Scenes from the Life of the People. Translated by Eric Bentley. *Modern Theater,* vol. I. Garden City: Doubleday Anchor Books, 1955.

Letters

Lettere al suo traduttore. A cura di Fredi Chiappelli. Firenze: Le Monnier, 1954.
Lettere a Dina. A cura di Gino Raya. Roma: Ciranna, 1962; new enlarged edition, retitled *Lettere d'amore,* 1971.
Lettere a Luigi Capuana. A cura di Gino Raya. Firenze: Le Monnier, 1975.
"Storia de *I Malavoglia:* carteggio con l'editore e con Luigi Capuana," con una notizia di L. e V. Perroni, *Nuova Antologia,* 16 marzo and 1 aprile 1940.

As to scattered letters that have appeared in journals, cf. the references in the notes.

SECONDARY SOURCES

ALEXANDER, ALFRED. *Giovanni Verga.* London: Grant & Cutler, 1972. A biography, which often appears to rest on gratuitous assumptions.
CATTANEO, GIULIO. *Verga.* Torino: UTET, 1963. By far the best Verga biography.
RAYA, GINO. *Bibliografia verghiana.* Roma: Ciranna, 1972. A very large, if incomplete, Verga bibliography.
SANTANGELO, GIORGIO. *Storia della critica verghiana.* Firenze: La Nuova Italia, 1962 [2nd edit.]. A brief but effective history of the Verga criticism.
SERONI, ADRIANO. *Verga.* Palermo: Palumbo, 1963. Another history of the Verga criticism—followed by a useful anthology.

The following list of critical studies is extremely limited.

ASOR ROSA, ALBERTO. *Il caso Verga.* Palermo: Palumbo, 1974. A number of contemporary critics analyze Verga's works from a mostly sociological standpoint.
BARSOTTI, ANNA. *Verga drammaturgo.* Firenze: La Nuova Italia, 1974. A close analysis of Verga's theater.

BERGIN, THOMAS G. *Giovanni Verga*. New Haven, Conn.: Yale University Press, 1931 (reissued by the Greenwood Press, Westport, Conn., 1969). To this day, the best work on Verga in English.

BIGAZZI, ROBERTO. *I colori del vero*. Pisa: Nistri-Lischi, 1969. A background book on the times of *verismo* and Verga.

BIGAZZI, ROBERTO. *Su Verga novelliere*. Pisa: Nistri-Lischi, 1975. Essays on Verga's major works.

CECCHETTI, GIOVANNI. *Il Verga maggiore*. Firenze: La Nuova Italia, 1968ff. Essays on the pivotal works in Verga's career.

CHIAPPELLI, FREDI. "Una lettura verghiana: 'La roba,'," *Letter Italiane*, XII (1960), 22–31; and "Una lettura verghiana: 'La lupa'," *Giornale storico della letteratura italiana*, CXXXIX (1962), 370–83. Two insightful stylistic analyses.

CONTINI, GIANFRANCO. *Giovanni Verga e il naturalismo regionale*, in *La letteratura italiana, Otto-Novecento*. Firenze: Sansoni, 1974. A condensed monograph of significance.

CROCE, BENEDETTO. *La letteratura della nuova Italia*, III, Bari Laterza (reprinted many times), 1–32. The essay that initiated serious Verga criticism.

DE BENEDETTI, GIACOMO. *Verga e il naturalismo*. Milano: Garzanti, 1976. A general book, mostly devoted to Verga's early novels and to the birth of his style.

DE ROBERTO, FEDERICO. *Casa Verga*, a cura di C. Musumarra. Firenze: Le Monnier, 1964. Indispensable biographical material.

GIACHERY, AMERICO. *Verga e D'Annunzio*. Milano: Silva, 1968. Good observations on Verga's style.

LUPERINI, ROMANO. *Pessimismo e verismo in Giovanni Verga*. Padova: Liviana, 1968; *L'orgoglio e la disperata rassegnazione*. Roma: Savelli, 1974; *Verga e le strutture narrative del realismo*. "Saggio su 'Rosso Malpelo.' " Padova: Liviana, 1976. From sociological (Marxist) views of Verga in general to more artistically oriented considerations.

MADRIGNANI, CARLO ALBERTO. *Capuana e il naturalismo*, Bari, Laterza, 1970. 1970. The best work on the theoretician of *verismo*.

MARCHI, GIANPAOLO. *Concordanze verghiane*. Verona:Fiorini, 1970. On the differences between the various versions of Verga's works.

MARIANI, GAETANO. *Storia della scapigliatura*. Caltanisetta-Roma: Sciascia, 1967. By far the best documented work on the Milanese group of writers and artists during the second half of the last century.

MARZOT, GIULIO. *Battaglie veristiche dell'Ottocento*. Milano-Messia: Principato, 1941. A reliable work on the *verismo* debates.

MASIELLO, VITILIO. *Il Verga tra ideologia e realta*. Bari: De Donato, 1972. A Marxist interpretation of our writer's personality as it emerges from his works.

MOMIGLIANO, ATTILIO. *Dante, Manzoni, Verga*. Messina-Firenze: D'Anna, 1944. A sensitive, although somewhat romantic, view of Verga's world.

MUSUMARRA, CARMELO. *Verga minore*, Pisa: Nistri-Lischi, 1965.
The first comprehensive study of Verga's early fiction.

NAVARRIA, AURELIO. *Lettura di poesia nell'opera di G. Verga*. Messina-
Firenze: D'Anna, 1962. A close, discriminating reading of most of
Verga's works.

NICOLOSI, FRANCESCO. *Questioni verghiane*. Roma: Edizioni dell'Ateneo,
1969. Two essays on Verga's formative years, and a study on the two
versions of *Mastro-don Gesualdo*.

RAGUSA, OLGA. *Verga's Milanese Tales*. New York: S. F. Vanni, 1964. The
only book-length essay on the subject. It also offers the translations of
several of Verga's prefaces (including the little-known alternate preface
to *I Malavoglia*) and of Pirandello's essay on Verga.

RAYA, GINO. *La lingua del Verga*. Firenze: Le Monnier, 1962. A study of
Verga's language with an explanation of the words peculiar to his texts.

RUSSO, LUIGI. *Giovanni Verga*. Bari: Laterza, 1947 [written in 1919, revised
in 1933, and with a 1941 essay on Verga's language; reprinted many
times]. The first and possibly the most important monograph on our
author.

SCRIVANO, RICCARDO. *La narrativa di Giovanni Verga*. Roma: Bulzoni, 1977.
A monograph that reinterprets and brings to maturity many critical
considerations. It also has a good bibliography.

SPITZER, LEO. "L'originalità della narrazione ne *I Malavoglia*," *Belfagor*, XI
(1956), 27–53. A fundamental essay for any study of Verga's style.

Index

Alexander, Alfred, 161n13
Abate, Antonino, 11, 12, 13
Aleardi, Aleardo, 17
Alfieri, Vittorio, 14
Alighieri, Dante, 11
Annoni, Carlo, 13, 155n4
Arbiter, Petronius, 45
Aretino, Pietro, 45
Ariosto, Ludovico, 11
Artuffo, Riccardo, 157n3
Assing, Ludmilla, 17

Bakunin, Mikhall, 17
Balzac, Honoré de, 46, 68
Barsotti, Anna, 161n9
Baudelaire, Charles, 20
Bergin, Thomas G., 7, 36, 96, 102, 150, 156n32, 159n8, 160n8, 161n10
Bernard, Claude, 47, 157n5
Biasin, Gian Paolo, 155n5
Bigazzi, Roberto, 31, 156n26, 158n8, 160n11
Boccaccio, Giovanni, 45, 125
Bohème, La (Puccini), 38, 153
Boito, Arrigo, 20, 149
Bonaparte, Napoleon, 12
Borgese, Maria, 157n6
Brigola, editore, 31

Cameroni, Felice, 47, 49
Capuana, Luigi, 17, 20, 36, 41, 45, 48, 49, 72, 96, 97, 98, 102, 156n30, 158n9, 159n11
Caracciolo dei Principi di Fiorino, Enrichetta, 18
Carcano, Giulio, 38
Carrer, Luigi, 18

Castellazzi di Sordevolo, Dina, 145, 146
Castorina, Domenico, 11, 12
Cattaneo, Giulio, 12, 155n2, 159n1, 161n14
Cecchetti, Giovanni, 157n34, 158n12, 159n7, 160n13, 161n5
Checchi, Tebaldo, 149
Chiappelli, Fredi, 158n13, 160n12
Cicognani, Bruno, 45
Coeur simple, Un (Flaubert), 118
Comte, August, 46, 70
Confessioni di un Italiano (Nievo), 22
Corriere della sera, 149, 157n1
Côte à Côte (Rod), 99
Cours de philosophie positive (Comte), 70
Croce, Benedetto, 31, 36, 97, 139, 156n20, 157n3, 159n18, 161n6

Dall'Ongaro, Francesco, 17, 18, 19, 20
D'Annunzio, Gabriele, 7, 45
Darwin, Erasmus, 46, 68, 70
D'Azeglio, Massimo, 12
De Benedetti, Giacomo, 31, 156n22
Del Balzo, Carlo, 97
Deledda, Grazia, 45
De Marchi, Emilio, 45
De Roberto, Federico, 7, 12, 18, 45, 147, 153, 154, 155n11, 161n12
De Sanctis, Francesco, 45, 46, 48, 51, 96, 157n4, 158n14, 159n12
Description, lack thereof, 75
Devoto, Giacomo, 159n9
Dialect, Sicilian, 14, 44–53
Dialogued narrative, 50; See also Free indirect speech
Diderot, Denis, 18

167

Donkeys, 64, 78, 80, 111–13
Dossi, Carlo, 20
Dumas, Alexandre, 12
Duse, Eleanora, 149

Economic factors. *See* Money

Farina, Salvatore, 20, 44
Flaubert, Gustave, 46, 102, 103, 118
Fojanesi, Giselda, 18, 145
Folklore elements, 38, 39, 42, 43, 53,
  54, 55, 63, 64, 87, 88, 89, 108, 125,
  130, 131, 153
Foscolo, Ugo, 11, 13, 14
Franchetti, Leopoldo, 96, 159n13
Free indirect speech, 30, 50, 58, 63, 94,
  145
Frères Zenganno, Les (Goncourt), 69
Fucini, Renato, 45
Fusinato, Arnaldo, 17

Garibaldi, Giuseppe, 11, 18, 73, 114
Garzanti, Livio, 128
Gattopardo, Il (Tomasi di Lampedusa),
  11
Germinie Lacerteux (Goncourt), 46
Giacosa, Giuseppe, 143, 149
Giolitti, Giovanni, 154
Goncourt, Edmond de, 46, 69, 70
Goncourt, Jules de, 46
Grossi, Tommaso, 18
Gualdo, Luigi, 149
Guerrazzi, Francesco Domenico, 12–13

Ildegonda (Grossi), 18
Italia contemporanea, L', 13

Language, 7, 26, 28, 30, 35, 37, 39,
  44–53, 54, 62, 63, 66, 71, 72, 76, 80,
  91, 95, 96, 97, 99, 105, 108, 115, 116,
  119, 127, 138, 147, 150
Lapp, John C., 157n5
Lo Nigro, Salvatore, 160n1
Lugli, Vittorio, 160n1
Luperini, Romano, 97, 141, 158n18,
  159n21, 161n1

Madame Bovary (Flaubert), 102, 103
Madrignani, Carlo A., 158n9

Maffei, Andrea, 17
Maffei Carrara-Spinelli, Clara, 20
Marcazzan, Mario, 158n8
Manzoni, Alessandro, 11, 14, 32, 45,
  154, 161n8
Marchi, Gian Paolo, 31, 156n27, 160n1
Mariani, Gaetano, 38, 155n13, 157n36
Martini, Ferdinando, 23, 156n18
Marzot, Giulio, 23, 120, 156n16, 158n8,
  160n16
Mascagni, Pietro, 56, 58, 146, 151, 152,
  153
Masiello, Vitilio, 158n12
Massarani, Tullo, 20
Menasci, Giovanni, 58, 151
Misteri del chiostro napoletano (Carac-
  ciolo dei Principi di Fiorino), 18
Momigliano, Attilio, 22, 139, 155n14,
  161n8
Money, 22, 35, 37, 38, 70, 78, 79, 81,
  82, 83, 86, 90, 101, 107, 108, 109, 110,
  111, 116, 117, 118, 122, 125, 128, 130,
  131, 132, 133, 134, 136, 138, 139, 143
Monleone, Domenico, 151
Monti, Vincenzo, 11
Murat, Joachim, 12, 13
Murger, Henri, 38
Musumarra, Carmelo, 16, 31, 155n8,
  156n23, 157n33

Nardi, Pietro, 155n13
Natio borgo selvaggio (Paolieri), 154
Naturalism, 44–53, 69; *See also* Verismo
Navarria, Aurelio, 17, 31, 155n10,
  156n24, 157n1
Nazione, La, 18
Negro, editore, 15
Niceforo, Niccolò, 13
Nicolosi, Francesco, 160n1
Nievo, Ippolito, 22, 32
Nuova Antologia, 23, 36, 45, 127, 147,
  156n29, 157n35, 159n1
Nuova Europa, La, 13

Ojetti, Ugo, 49 157n7, 158n10

Pancrazi, Pietro, 157n7
Paola, Salvatore, 68, 69, 127

Paolieri, Ferdinando, 154
Partita a scacchi, Una (Giacosa), 143
Pascoli, Giovanni, 45
Pasolini, Pier Paolo, 7
Pavese, Cesare, 7
Pecoto, Caterina, 18, 19
Perroni, Lina, 13, 122, 157n35, 158n16, 159n4n6n1
Perroni, Vito, 122, 157n35, 158n16n18, 159n4n6n1
Pescatori, Salvatore, 159n16
Petrarch, Francesco, 11, 45, 46, 48
Petronio, Giuseppe, 161n4
Piccioni, Leone, 160n1
Pirandello, Luigi, 7, 45, 143, 144, 145, 154
Pitré, Giuseppe, 157n8
Popular narrative, 49, 63, 71
Praga, Emilio, 20
Prati, Giovanni, 17
Profumo (Capuana), 48
Proverbs, 75, 76, 78, 81, 82, 93
Promessi sposi, I (Manzoni), 14, 18
Puccini, Giacomo, 38, 153

Ragonese, Gaetano, 17, 155n9, 157n33
Ragusa, Olga, 40, 157n37, 160n15
Ragusa-Moleti, Girolamo, 157n8
Rapisardi, Mario, 18, 145
Raya, Gino, 156n15, 161n15
Religieuse, La (Diderot), 18
"religione della famiglia," 42, 43
Risorgimento, 12
Rivista minima, 44
Rod, Edouard, 56, 97, 99, 129, 146
Roma degli Italiani, 13
Romanò, Angelo, 155n13
Rosa, Alberto Asor, 158n12
Rossi, Cesare, 149
Russo, Luigi, 7, 16, 19, 31, 57, 97, 102, 124, 139, 155n7, 156n21, 158n8n11-n17, 159n19, 160n9n18, 161n7n11

Scapigliatura, 20, 32, 38, 45, 46, 155n13
Scarfoglio, Edoardo, 159n10
Scènes de la vie bohème (Murger), 38
Scrivano, Riccardo, 31, 156n25
Serao, Matilde, 45

Sexuality, 15, 53–56, 88–90; *See also* Folklore elements
Sociological approach *(Malavoglia, Mastro-don Gesualdo)*, 70, 84, 85, 86, 88, 89, 97, 101, 115, 128, 139
Sonnino, Sidney, 96, 159n13
Sonzogno, Edoardo, 151
Sordevolo, Count Brucco, 146
Spitzer, Leo, 158n12, 159n20
Style, 7, 12, 14, 25, 27, 33, 35, 37, 41, 42, 44–53, 55, 57, 61, 65, 71, 77, 80, 86, 91–97, 98, 103, 105, 107, 128, 138, 145, 148
Suora, La (Carrer), 18
Svevo, Italo, 7

Taine, Hippolyte A., 46
Tarchetti, Iginio, 38
Targioni-Tozzetti, Giovanni, 58
Tasca, Pierantonio, 161n14
Theater, 17, 18, 56, 58, 118, 144, 148–54
Thérèse Raquin (Zola), 46, 157n5
Tomasi di Lampedusa, Giuseppe, 11
Torelli-Viollier, Eugenio, 149, 151
Torraca, Francesco, 96, 97, 159n14
Torrisi, Mario, 12
Tasso, Torquato, 11
Tozzi, Federico, 45
Treves, Emilio, 20, 37, 75, 128, 147, 149, 157n35
Trombatore, Gaetano, 158n9
Trovarsi (Pirandello), 143

Ultime lettere di Jacopo Ortis (Foscolo), 13

Verga, Giovanni
  WORKS–DRAMA:
  Caccia al lupo, La (The Wolf Hunt), 153–54
  Caccia alla volpe, La (The Fox Hunt), 153–54
  Cavalleria rusticana, 146, 149–52
  Dal tuo al mio (What's Yours Is Mine), 147–48, 156n28, 161n7
  Lupa, La (The She-wolf), 152–53, 161n14
  Portineria, In (The Porter's Lodgings), 118, 152

Rose caduche (Fading Roses), 17, 149, 161n9

WORKS–FICTION:

"Agonia di un villaggio, L' " (The Agony of a Village), 125

"Amante di Gramigna, L' " (Gramigna's Lover), 44–53, 55, 69, 71, 72, 99

"Amante di Raia, L' " (Raia's Lover), 44

Amore e patria (Love and Country), 12

"Amore senza benda" (Love without Veils), 118

"Artisti da strapazzo" (Drifting Artists), 123–24

"Barberina di Marcantonio, La" (Marcantonio's Little Barbara), 122

"Bastione di Monforte, Il" (The Monforte Rampart), 117

"Bell'Armando, Il" (Handsome Armand), 124

"Bollettino sanitario" (Medical Bulletin), 121

"Caccia al lupo, La" (The Wolf Hunt), 153–54

"Camerati" (Buddies), 120

"Canarino del N. 15, Il" (The Canary of No. 15), 117–18, 151

"Capanna e il tuo cuore, Una" (In a Hut with your Heart), 154

Carbonari della montagna, I (The Mountain Carbonari), 12, 13, 155n4

"Cavalleria rusticana," 30, 56–58, 59, 116, 123, 142, 149

"Certi argomenti" (A Certain kind of Reasoning), 40

"Chiave d'oro, La" (The Gold Key), 122

"Coda del diavolo, La" (The Tricks of Life), 30–40, 41

"Come, il quando ed il perché, Il" (The How, the When and the Wherefore), 66, 103–104, 116, 121

"Conforti" (Consolation), 119–20

"Cos'è il re" (So Much for the King), 115

Dal tuo al mio (What's Yours Is Mine), 147–48, 156n28, 161n7

"Di lá dal mare" (Across the Sea), 116

Don Candeloro & C., 141–45, 156n28

"Don Licciu Papa," 116, 122

"Dramma intimo" (Personal Drama), 121

"Drammi ignoti" (Unknown Dramas), 121

Drammi intimi (Personal Dramas), 121–22, 141

Duchessa di Gargantas (Duchess of Gargantas), 69

Duchessa di Leyra, La (The Duchess of Leyra), 69, 72, 141, 142, 145–47

"Epopea spicciola" (Plain Epic), 144

Eros, 25–31, 32, 33, 37, 43, 48, 53, 98, 103, 121, 156n19, 160n3

Eva, 20–23, 32, 35, 48, 155n6, 156n18

"Fantasticheria" (Images), 42–43, 44, 116, 158n18

"Festa dei morti, La" (All Soul's Day), 125

"Fra le scene della vita" (Behind the Curtains of Life), 144

"Galantuomini, I" (Gentry), 116

"Gelosia" (Jealousy), 119

"Guerra di Santi" (War between Saints), 65–67

"Innamorati, Gl' " (The Lovers), 142, 144

"Jeli il pastore" (Ieli), 36, 59–63, 114, 123

"Lacrymae rerum" (The Tears of Things), 125

Lettere a Dina (Letters to Dina), 156n15, 160n6, 161n3n4n5

Lettere a Luigi Capuana (Letters to Luigi Capuana), 156n17, 157n2, 159n3n15n2, 160n7n10

Lettere al suo traduttore (Letters to his Translator), 158n13, 159n2n17, 160n4, 161n3n5

Lettere d'amore (Love Letters), 156n15, 160n6, 161n3n5

"Libertà" (Freedom), 104, 114–15, 120, 160n14

"Lupa, La" (The She-Wolf), 36, 49, 53–56, 57, 59

"Maestro dei ragazzi, Il" (The Teacher), 125

"Malaria," 105–107

Malavoglia, I (The House by the Medlar Tree), 24, 30, 36, 37, 38, 43, 51, 56, 67, 68–97, 98, 104, 111, 117, 124, 127, 129, 132, 138, 139, 140, 146, 157n35, 158n12n18, 159n4n5-n6n14n1

Marea, La (The Tide), 68

"Marionette parlanti, Le" (Talking Puppets), 142–43

Marito di Elena, Il (Helen's Husband), 98–103, 117, 156n19, 160n11

Mastro-don Gesualdo, 69, 72, 97, 109, 115, 122, 127–40, 141, 142, 143, 145, 160n1n2, 161n5

"Mistero, Il" (The Mystery Play), 116

"Nanni Volpe," 124–25

"Nedda," 26, 31–37, 48, 104, 156n28

Novelle (Stories), 37, 156n28

Novelle rusticane (Rustic Tales), 104–17, 118, 121, 123, 124, 145, 156n28

Nuovi Tartufi, I (The New Tartuffes), 149

Onorevole Scipioni, L', 69

"Opera del Divino Amore, L'" (The Society of Divine Love), 142, 143

"Orfani, Gli" (The Orphans), 113–14

"Osteria dei 'Buoni Amici', L'" (The "Good Friends" Inn), 119

Pardon 'Ntoni (I Malavoglia), 37, 38, 41, 42, 68, 72, 73, 75, 158n18

"Paggio Fernando" (Page Fernando), 143

"Pane nero" (Black Bread), 101, 110–11, 123, 160n13

"Papa Sisto", 142, 143, 144

"Peccato di Donna Santa, Il" (Lady Santa's Sin), 144

Peccatrice, Una (A Sinner), 14–17, 19, 21, 29, 33, 35, 54, 149, 155n6

"Pentolaccia" (Stinkpot), 65–67, 116, 158n19

Per le vie (Through the Streets), 38, 117–21, 125, 145, 151, 156n28

"Piazza della Scala, In" (La Scala Square), 117

Primavera ed altri racconti (Springtime and Other Tales), 37–40, 41, 119

"Processo, Un" (A Trial), 124

"Quelli del colera" (Cholera Times), 125

"Reverendo, Il" (The Reverend Father), 115, 122, 142

Ricordi del Capitano D'Arce, I (Captain D'Arce's Recollections), 122, 141–145, 156n28

"Roba, La" (Property), 107–10, 111, 124, 136

"Rosso Malpelo," 63–65, 113, 158n18

"Segno d'amore, Il" (The Mark of Love), 124

"Semplice storia" (A Simple Tale), 118–19

"Serata della diva, La" (The Star's Great Night), 143

"Storia dell'asino di San Giuseppe" (Story of the Saint Joseph Donkey), 111–13

Storia di una capinera (Story of a Blackcap), 117–20, 142, 155n6

"Storie del castello di Trezza, Le" (The Ghosts of Trezza Castle), 38–39

Sulle lagune (On the Lagoon), 13, 14, 155n5

"Tentazione" (Temptation), 121–22

Tigre reale (Royal Tigress), 23–25, 26, 29, 40, 48, 53, 54, 141, 149, 155n6

"Tramonto di Venere, Il" (The Setting of Venus), 143

Tutte le novelle, 122m 156n28, 159n19, 160n5n17

"Ultima giornata, L'" (The Last Day), 120–21

"Ultima visita, L'" (The Last Visit), 121

"Ultima volta, L'" (The Last Time), 121

Uomo di lusso, L', 69

Vagabondaggio (Wanderers), 122–26, 156n28, 160n17

"Veglione, Al" (At the Masked Ball), 117

"Via Crucis" (The Calvary Road), 119

Vinti, I (The Doomed), 30, 68, 98, 110, 115, 127, 140, 141, 158n18

Vita dei campi (Life in the Fields), 36,

37, 40, 41–67, 103, 104, 116, 117,
123, 124, 138, 145, 156n28, 157n34,
158n12, 159n20
"Vocazione di Suora Agnese, La" (Sister Agnes's Vocation), 142, 143
"X" (The Mark X), 40
Verismo, 32, 36, 44–53, 73, 158n8

Vico, Giambattista, 46

Wagner, Wilhelm Richard, 20

Zola, Emile, 32, 46, 47, 48, 68, 157n4n5,
158n14, 159n12